THEN AND THERE SERIES
GENERAL EDITOR
MARJORIE REEVES

D1798933

The Last Fighting Indians of the American West

B W BEACROFT

Illustrated from contemporary sources

LONGMAN

LONGMAN GROUP LIMITED
London
Associated companies, branches and representatives
throughout the world

© Longman Group Ltd 1976
All rights reserved. No part of this publication
may be reproduced, stored in a retrieval system,
or transmitted in any form or by any means, electronic,
mechanical, photocopying, recording or otherwise,
without the prior permission of the copyright owner.

First published 1976
ISBN 0 582 20538 7

Filmset in Hong Kong by Asco Trade Typesetting Limited
Printed in Hong Kong by Sheck Wah Tong Printing Press

Contents

To the Reader

Little more than a hundred years ago most Indians living west of the mighty Mississippi River were still free people. On the grassy plains Indians like the Teton Sioux and the Cheyennes hunted the buffalo. In the hot south-west the Apache tribes were warlike and added to their possessions by stealing and plundering from the Indian and Mexican settlements around them. In the thickly wooded valleys and grassy plains of the north between two mountain ranges lived the Nez Perće Indians.* They hunted *elk* and deer, trapped smaller game, fished for salmon, and gathered fruits and berries. The map in the inside cover of this book shows the homelands of these Indian tribes.

These Indian ways of life, however, were near their end. The white man's interest in the Indian country was growing. Explorers, fur traders and mountainmen spent much time in the Far West between 1800 and 1850. By 1850 wagon trains of settlers and miners were crossing the plains and mountains on their way to California and Oregon and by 1870 railroad men and cattle ranchers followed. Sometimes the Indians attacked the white strangers: often they traded with them. But soon the white man came to want Indian country for himself. Soldiers came with orders to place the Indians on reservations and kill all those who resisted the white man. The advance of the Americans across the plains, mountains and deserts west of the River Mississippi is described in detail by Barbara Currie in two other Then and There books: 'Pioneers in the American West 1780–1840', and 'Railroads and Cowboys in the American West'.

Many Indians were overcome quickly and without force. The Teton Sioux, the Nez Percés and the Apaches resisted the white man as fiercely as they could. This book tells something of the early lives of these peoples, the wars they fought against the white man, and what the white Americans did with them at the end of the nineteenth century.

*Nez Percé is a French term which means 'pierced nose'. Pronounce like this – Nay Pair-say. The reason why these Indians got such a name is explained on page 17.

Words printed in *italics* in the text are explained in the Glossary, p. 94.

1   The Apaches: Raiders of the South-west

The American South-west is a land of mountains and deserts. Snow and ice covers the mountain slopes for part of the year. In summer the streams flow fast and clear, the valleys and hillsides have grassy meadows, and the pine forests give cool shade from the bright sun. The mountains rise up out of deserts of sand and rock, barren except for prickly, fleshy and deep-rooted plants like the cactus and the mesquite. On the desert floors live rattlesnakes and lizards, kangaroo rats and horned toads – the only creatures which can endure the dry, scorching heat; all, that is, except the Apaches who used to live in these burning wastelands.

Map 2 shows the area of the Apache homeland and shows the homes of those tribes which will be mentioned in this book – the Mescaleros, the Mimbrenos, the Chiricahuas and the Jicarillas.

Britton Davis, a soldier who fought against the Apaches in the 1880s, described their appearance:

They were of medium height, few over five feet eight, but proportioned like deer. Small hands and feet; small bones; thin arms and legs, the latter sinewed as though with steel cords, so taut were the *sinews* and devoid of fat. Chests broad, deep and full, the *heritage* from generations of mountain-dwelling ancestors, they moved along the trail with a smooth, effortless stride that seemed as tireless as a machine and as rhythmical.

The Apaches had broad, round and rather flat faces. They grew their hair long and were proud of it. Sometimes it was

5

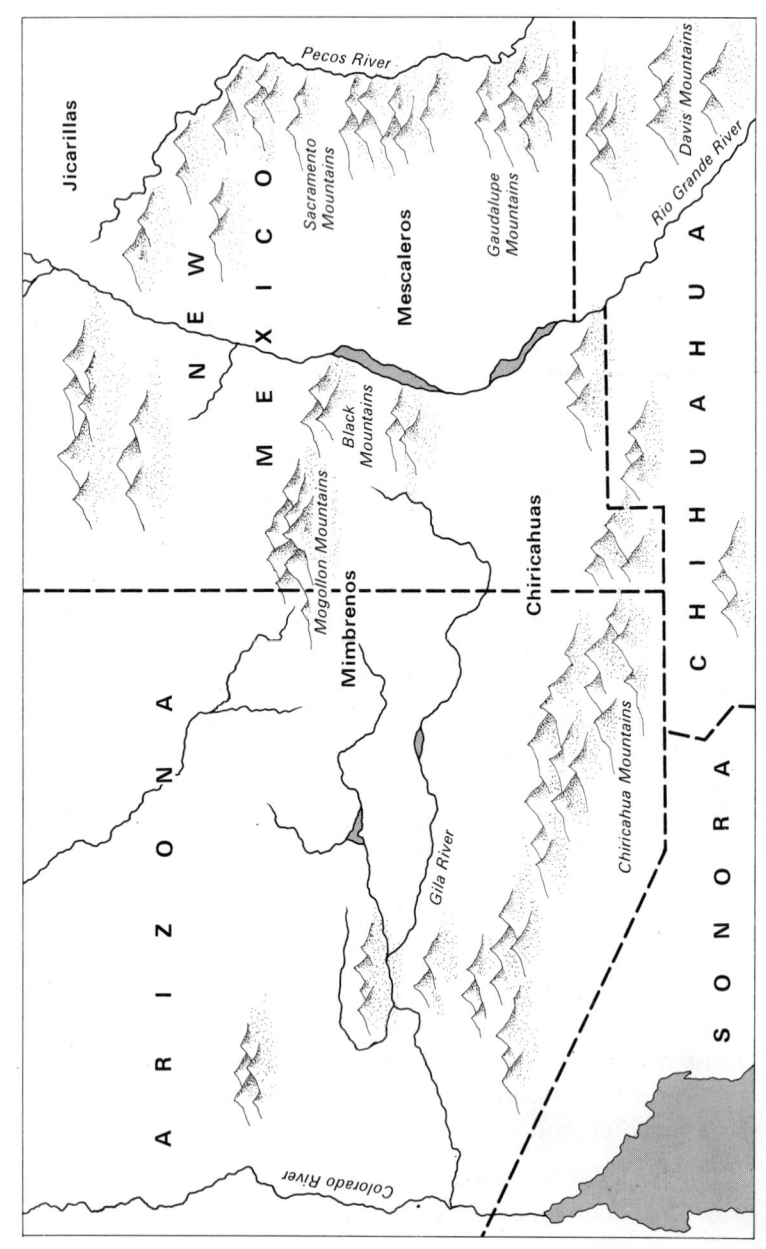

MAP 2   *The Apache homeland*

6

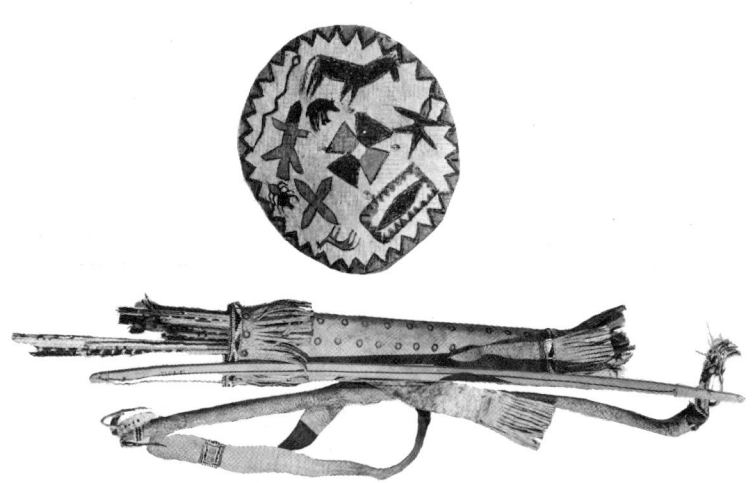

The shield, quiver, bows and arrows of the Mescalero

braided, but usually it hung loose down to the shoulders. The hair was kept out of the eyes by headbands of red cloth.

The men wore long, brightly coloured shirts and *breechclouts*, the women long dresses. For all the Apaches, however, the most important single item of clothing was the high moccasin, a shoe and legging combined in one. This was very necessary. Without moccasins their feet and legs would have been torn and swollen by the spikes and thorns of the cactus and mesquite

In the summer the Apaches camped among the cool pines and green meadows of the mountains. Hunting was good. On the high slopes the men killed elk and *mule deer*. Lower down and out on the plains to the east, they shot white-tailed deer and antelope. Usually the hunters worked in groups, finding and surrounding the herd, and then closing up within the shooting range of their bows and arrows. Sometimes a skilful hunter worked alone, wearing an animal skin over his head and shoulders, stalking his prey, moving on all fours and imitating its sounds and movements. In this way, a man could often get very close to the herd and kill an animal before it sensed the danger. Parties of hunters also journeyed to the high plains in the east to hunt buffalo. Both men and women went, the men 7

to do the killing and the women to cut up the meat.

The cold snows of the winter forced the Apaches to move down to the deserts and plains of the Southwest. There the game was more scarce. Rabbits and wild turkeys were hunted as well as deer. If the meat supplies were very low the tribes would even shoot rats, mice, lizards and rattlesnakes. All meat was cooked and, when not eaten immediately, was cut into strips, smoked over the fires, and stored away until needed.

While the men hunted for game the women searched for other foods in the wilderness. They gathered sun-flower seeds, wild onions and wild potatoes. Fruits were taken from the cactuses and the yucca plants. When dried they were like figs. Wild honeycombs hung high on the cliffs. These were shot down by arrows, the women catching them on skins as they fell. The Apaches stored the honey in leather bags and valued it greatly.

The mescal plant was especially important to these Indians. The Mescalero Apaches are thought to take their name from it. Groups of women would search for the mescal plants, sometimes as thick and tall as telegraph poles. Working with hatchets and sticks with chisel-shaped ends the women cut down the plant and chopped off its long fleshy leaves and large white head. Each head was about a metre in diameter and about a ton of them were placed together. Then a pit was dug, about 3 metres long and over a metre wide and deep, and lined with stones. Hot coals were lit, mats of vegetation spread over them, and the mescal heads were cooked for several days. The leaves of the mescal stuck out from the pit, their fleshy ends cooking with the heads. From time to time the women pulled out a leaf and tasted it. When the taste was right the pit was uncovered and the mescal taken out. It was sweet and delicious. Uneaten mescal was sliced like cheese and dried on flat rocks for use later. With a handful of mescal and some dried meat from a deer an Apache could run and walk all day long.

Left: *This photograph shows very well what the Apache warrior looked like, the sort of clothes he wore, and the kinds of weapons he used*   9

From the mescal, too, the Indian made thread, sandals and bags.

No other Indians had such knowledge of desert plants. The Mescaleros are said to have made use of at least one hundred different plants in their daily lives. Knowledge like this was an important reason why the Apaches could survive in the desert when no other men could.

But they were not simply hunters and gatherers. They were fierce raiders, attacking the settlements round them, stealing and killing. For hundreds of years Apache warriors had robbed the Pueblo Indians who lived near them, taking their food, clothes and weapons and enslaving their women and children. Later, when the Spaniards came, Apaches often raided their ranches, driving off their horses and cattle. It was from the Spaniards that the Apaches first learned to ride horses. Once they had horses they were never without again. When they needed more, the Apaches stole them from the whites.

The Apaches did not see anything wrong in raiding and plundering their neighbours. Their forefathers had done it. It was part of their normal life. To capture things from the Pueblos or the Spaniards showed cunning and bravery and the tribe lived better because it had more food or weapons.

Nobody could stay alive in the desert except an Apache. Walking and running he could cover 100 kilometres a day if necessary. He could carry his water supply inside a long animal *intestine* wrapped round his waist. The Apache could go twice as long without food and four times as long without water as any of his enemies.

At certain times in the history of America the Apache raids were so damaging to the white man that he was forced to do something very severe to try to stop the attacks. For example, the northern provinces of Mexico decided to wipe out the Apaches. They promised to pay a hundred dollars for the scalp of each Apache man, twenty-five dollars for a woman's, and ten for a child's. White men became scalp hunters. Some used unfair and cruel methods to kill the Apaches. In 1837, a white trapper named Johnson invited some Mimbreno

An engraving by Frederic Remington showing Apaches returning from a raid in Mexico. Remington spent many years out west and became famous for his illustrations of western life. Most of them are scenes of excitement, adventure, danger, action, violence and death

Apaches to feast at a town called Santa Rita del Cobra. He then got busy:

> To one side of the ground where his feast was spread he placed a *howitzer*, loaded to the muzzle with *slugs*, nails and bullets, and concealed under sacks of flour and other goods. In good range he placed a sack of flour which he told the Indians to divide amongst themselves. Unsuspicious of wrong, they gathered about it. Johnson touched his lighted

cigarillo to the vent of the howitzer and the charge was poured into the crowd, killing and wounding many.

Such methods only made the Apache raids worse. Can you think why?

Apaches were taught how to hunt and fight and survive in the wilderness from a very early age. Young Apache boys and girls were given bows and arrows as soon as they were old enough to use them. They practised their weapons daily, hunting for rabbits, squirrels, grouse and prairie chickens. In the winter they bathed in ice-covered rivers. In the summer they ran long distances carrying water in their mouths. At the end of their run they had to spit out the water. As they grew up the young were expected to learn how to behave. Until they had learned this they did not receive their Apache name. Kaywaykla, an Apache, was called by the Spanish name of Torres while he was young. He asked his grandmother how he could earn an Apache name. She said:

> First by obedience. An Apache obeys or dies. Not only his life but that of the tribe may depend upon his obedience and his truthfulness.
>
> . . . Above all, you must be truthful. If you are, you will be respected; and without respect no human relationship is of any value. . . . The liar is despised by all. And you must be useful and observant. You see how the older boys compete for the honour of serving the warriors. They care for the horses, run the errands, cook the food, and try to *anticipate* and supply the needs of him whom they serve. They listen respectfully and ask no questions unless they are necessary for obeying commands. They eat poor food, fast for long intervals, are faithful in every way, and above all, do not discuss things they may overhear.

Kaywaykla was a very respectable name: it meant 'His Enemies Lie Dead in Heaps'.

The Apaches lived in houses called 'wickiups'. They were small and *dome-shaped*, and made by placing animal skins over a rough framework of sticks, saplings or brush. The entrance was low and protected from the wind by brush piled up in front of it. Inside, in the centre, there was a fireplace, and the smoke escaped through a hole in the roof. Skins or pine needles served as bedding. If the Apaches were on a raid or knew enemies were close by they would build very crude wickiups in a few minutes, using whatever wood and brush they could find.

A group of Apaches who roamed the Gila River before settling down at a *reservation* called Ojo Caliente (Warm Springs) in New Mexico were known as the Warm Springs Apaches. These people worshipped Ussen, the Creator of Life. It was Ussen, they believed, who had made the mountains, streams, forests and deserts, and who had given the Apaches their land. Apache chiefs like Victorio and Nana are said to have prayed to him each day of their lives.

They believed that the son of Ussen, called Child of the Waters, had lived a life of much strife. He had fought and killed the Giant Buffalo, the Giant Bear, the Giant Deer and the Giant Owl. As a boy he had slain the terrible Yehyeh, a monster in human form who wanted to eat all the Apache people. The monster's arrows all splintered and broke before they reached Child of the Waters, yet the Boy's grass arrows pierced the stone armour of the Yehyeh and entered its heart. However, although the monster was dead, it had left a family living in a crater at the top of a mountain. Like the monster, all the members of its family had the power to kill Apaches simply by looking at them. Child of the Waters was carried to the mountain top by his friend, the Giant Lizard. Down into the crater Child of the Waters emptied a bag of powder which made the fire in the bottom burn with great flames and fumes. All the evil creatures were blinded. Child of the Waters then shot and killed them with his arrows. After his life was over he joined his father, Ussen, in the Happy Land. To the Apaches the life of Child of the Waters had a real meaning. Like him, all Apaches faced lives of struggle and difficulty. It was not good for people to have an easy life. All Apaches must conquer their enemies. They prayed to him for the strength and courage to do it.

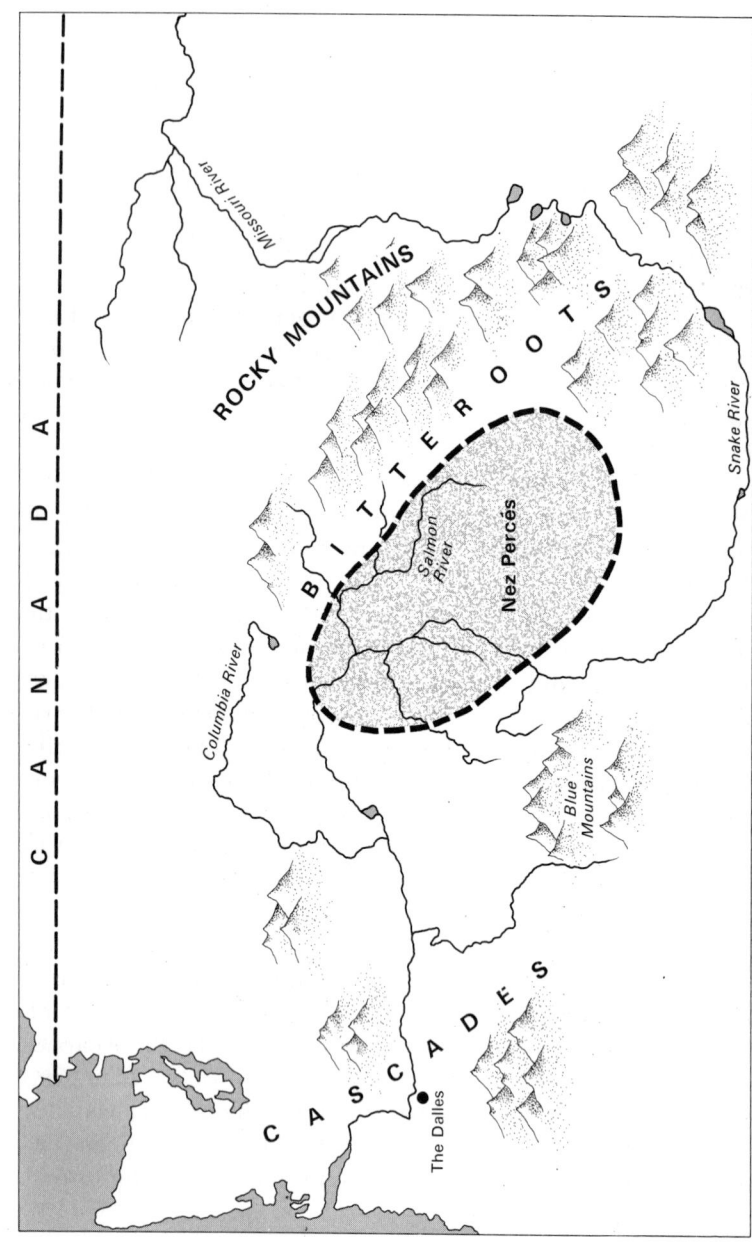

MAP 3 *The Nez Percé homeland*

2 The Nez Percés: Mountain Indians of the North-west

The Nez Percé Indians lived in the north-west corner of America, between the Cascades and the Rocky Mountains, between the border with Canada and the curving Snake River to the south. Their homeland is shown on map 3. It was a land of snow-capped peaks, forests and meadows, steep valleys and *canyons*, high plains and narrow ridges. Clouds and fogs often hid the mountain tops, the winters were cold, and the snows often came suddenly.

Many centuries ago, said Nez Percé legend, before any Indians lived, a giant sea monster had come to live in the Kamiah valley near the Clearwater River. It was so huge that it filled the entire valley, trampling down all the grass and trees and eating all the animals. One animal, the *coyote*, was determined to kill the monster. Together with his friend the fox, they thought of a way to do it. First, they got friendly with the sea creature and then, one day while it was eating, the coyote crept into its mouth and went down into the monster's chest. There, with five sharp flints, the coyote cut away its heart and the monster fell dead.

From the huge body the coyote and the fox made the first Indians. They made the Blackfoot people out of the monster's feet and the Flathead Indians from its head. Many other tribes were made until there was nothing left of the monster. Then the fox said that they had forgotten to make people for the Kamiah valley, which was the most beautiful of all the lands on earth. Saying nothing, the coyote shook his paw, still dripping with blood from the sea monster's heart, and from the final red drops they made the Nez Percés, the noblest of all the

Indians.

Like all Indians, the Nez Percé believed himself a natural part of his surroundings. He was a brother to the animals and trees, the flowers and the birds, the wind and the rain. The earth was his mother. From her came the land, food, water, clothes – everything the Nez Percé needed to live his life. He believed, too, that there were spirits everywhere: in the thunder and lightning, in the streams and rivers, and in all living creatures. It was very important to him to make contact with at least one of these spirits and to win its protection. To have his own guardian spirit was to have *Wyakin*: it would protect him from evil and bad luck and give him help when he needed it.

Early in life, between about nine and fourteen years of age, the young Nez Percé boy or girl would go to a lonely place and sit without food or water for perhaps several days. In that wild place the young Indian would feel the heat of the sun and the cold of the night, hear the crash of thunder and the howl of wolves and coyotes, or see the dark silhouette of a grizzly bear. Any of these things could mean that a spirit had come to see him. If the spirits of thunder and lightning spoke to him it meant he would be brave in battle, if that of a grizzly bear, it meant he would be very strong.

Once a spirit had spoken with the young Indian he left the wild place and returned to the village. In winter time, at the Guardian Spirit Dance, he would join the circle of dancers and sing the song his guardian spirit had taught him. The audience would hear clues to the nature of his Wyakin in the words he chanted. If a wolf spirit was the Wyakin, then the word wolf would be repeated again and again. From this time on the young Indian would call himself by the name of his guardian spirit. For the rest of his life he would keep a small bag by his side all the time. It would contain small things which reminded him of his guardian spirits; for example, bird's feathers and claws, pieces of fur, or a piece of bark struck by lightning.

White men first met the Nez Percés about the beginning of the nineteenth century. At this time the tribe numbered

A Nez Percé Indian

between 4,000 and 6,000 people, scattered in many small villages along the Snake River and the rivers and streams that emptied into it.

The homes were made by digging out circular or rectangular holes in the ground, banking up the earth round the holes, and then roofing the enclosed space with poles, earth, reeds and grass. Other houses were much bigger. They were built in the same way but were perhaps 30 metres in length and several families all lived together inside. These were called long houses. Fires burned along the centre of each house, the smoke escaping through holes in the roof.

In 1805 Lewis and Clark, two American explorers, met the Nez Percés. In their reports they said these Indians wore clothes made from the skins and furs of buffalo, elk and goat. Both men and women decorated their clothes with beads, sea shells and bits of bones. The men even used these things to decorate their hair. About this time some French trappers noticed that some of these Indians wore pieces of shell in their noses. They called them the Nez-Percé Indians and this is the name they have been known by ever since.

To keep themselves alive the Nez Percés hunted deer, elk, bear and mountain sheep, and fished for salmon. In the springtime the entire village climbed to the high meadows to dig up roots called kouse which were pounded into large cakes, dried in the sun, and then either eaten as bread or boiled to make a mushy soup. In the following months the people also gathered other roots, nuts and berries. By late June the 17

A photograph of Jason, an old Nez Percé, taken in 1868. Notice the use of furs, skins and feathers in the making of his clothes

meadows were full of camas flowers. The Indians dug up the camas roots, which looked like small onions, and ate them raw or cooked. They had a sweet taste. The camas harvest was a happy time. The women worked in the meadows while the men hunted and played games. Food was not always plentiful. Winter time was often a time of hunger. If the supplies of camas and dried meat ran out the Indians were forced to eat mosses and fibre from the bark of trees.

The Nez Percés also conducted trade with many neighbouring tribes. Their favourite place of trade was at the Dalles, westwards on the River Columbia. Here, at a spot where the river charged through rocky narrows, Indians from all over the north-west made their camps.

From the Shoshonis to the south-east the Nez Percés got their first horses. The date is unknown but it was probably about 1750. These animals changed their lives. Now they had a good means of moving their possessions and themselves over the rugged land. Horses meant they could travel faster and further. They became real assets in hunting. More and more Nez Percé men began to travel east through the mountains to the buffalo country of the high plains.

As their horse herds grew, more and more Nez Percés loaded up their animals with dried salmon, nuts and berries, camas roots, shells from the Dallas, and bows made of horn. They travelled to the buffalo country where they traded with the Flathead, the Shoshoni and the Blackfoot Indians. The fishing villages of the Nez Percés grew wealthier, their food supplies increased and their lives became more comfortable.

The buffalo country was a dangerous place. The Blackfoot and the Gros Ventres Indians, who received guns from the British and French traders, began to make war on other tribes, stealing their trade goods and horses and striking terror amongst them. Nez Percé traders did not escape these attacks. When the news reached back to their fishing villages Nez Percé men formed war parties to ride east and take revenge on their enemies. Each warrior painted a yellow, red, green or black pattern on his eyelids, cheeks and body which represented his own guardian spirit. Thick orange or red dye was painted heavily on his forehead to give him strength. Even his horse was painted. On the head and neck he painted lines of yellow and red. The mane was darkened and the body decorated with stripes, circles and zigzag lines. From the horse's head and tail trailed colourful feathers and streamers.

The main object of the war party was to surprise an enemy camp and drive off the horses. Hand to hand fighting was rare. Touching an enemy and escaping to tell the tale around the village camp fire led to much boasting and was thought to be a great feat. Sometimes fierce fighting was unavoidable. Scalps and prisoners were taken. Back in the Nez Percé villages the prisoners were tortured by the women for several days. They then became slaves but were treated kindly and quite often adopted by a Nez Percé family.

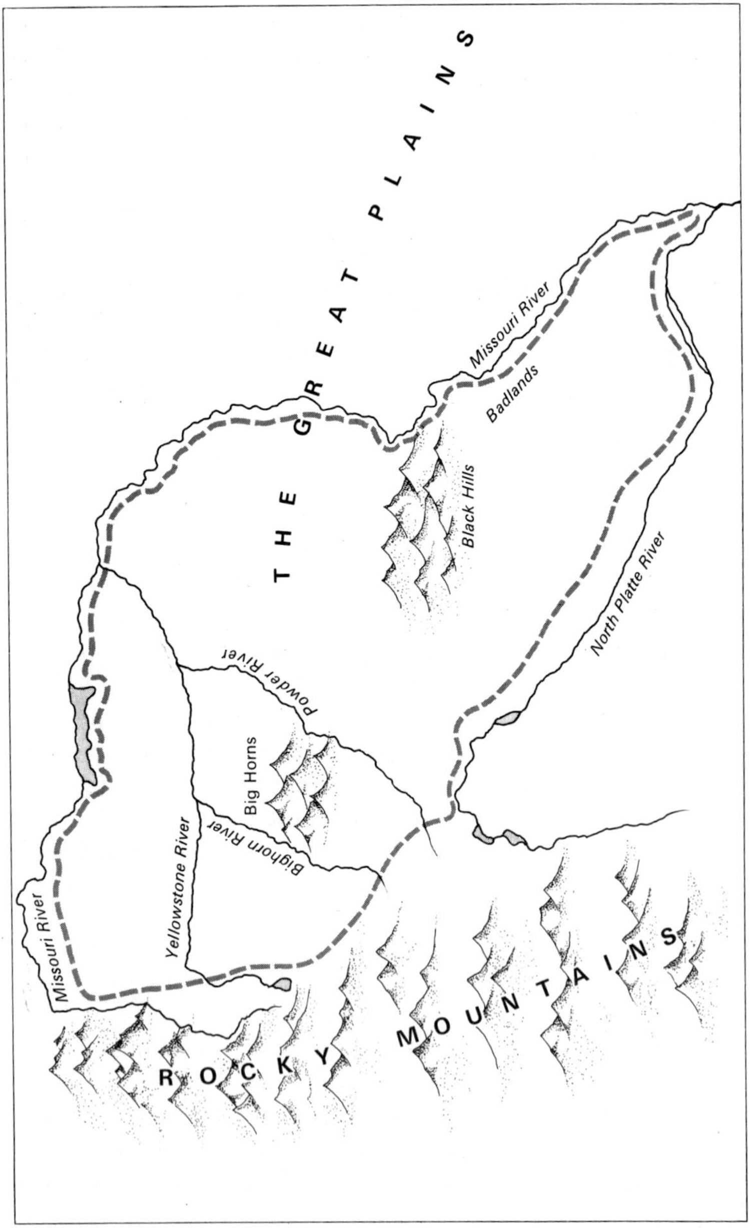

MAP 4 *The hunting grounds of the Teton Sioux*

3   The Teton Sioux: Buffalo Hunters of the Plains

About 1850 the most powerful Indian nation on the great plains was the Teton Sioux, or Dacota. Numbering perhaps 10,000 people the Dacota were split into several tribes: the Hunkpapa, the Oglala, the Brulé, the Sans Arc and the Miniconjou. Like the other plains Indians the Sioux were continually following the vast buffalo herds on which their lives depended. Map 4 shows roughly the area of their hunting grounds. They had lived here since about 1750, at

Tipis on the Plains. This finely detailed illustration is by Karl Bodmer who travelled with a German scientific expedition across the plains between 1832 and 1834. These tipis belonged to Assiniboin Indians but were very much like those of the Sioux

first hunting on foot. By 1800 the Sioux had obtained horses, by trade and by stealing, and they had become mighty hunters and warriors. There were two great hunts each year – in spring and autumn. At these times the families of a tribe would camp altogether, their *tipis* placed in a great semicircle on a valley floor. Each tipi was made by long poles covering with ten to twenty buffalo hides neatly sewn together and tailored to fit the frame. Brightly painted skins lined the inside. Skins also covered the floor, except where the fire was made. The tipi was easy to put up and take down, very weatherproof, roomy, warm in winter and cool in summer. Many hundreds, even a thousand tipis or lodges, might be found together. Once the buffalo herds were sighted the discipline in the camp became strict. The tribe worked as a team. Anyone disobeying orders and frightening away a herd could be killed or have all his possessions burned.

The hunting was done in various ways. One method was for the hunters, armed with short bows, to run their ponies close behind the fleeing buffalo and fire their arrows up behind the short ribs and into the heart or lungs. The expert hunter only needed one shot to make a kill.

Another way was for hunters to surround a herd, close in, and kill as many buffalo as they could with arrows and lances before the terrified animals broke out of the hunters' circle. This was dangerous work but the Indians were very quick when something went wrong. In 1832 a white man watching this kind of hunt wrote that the wounded and maddened buffalo

> turned on their *assailants*, and many warriors who were dismounted saved themselves by the superior muscles of their legs. Some who were closely pursued by the bulls wheeled suddenly and, snatching the part of the buffalo robe from their waists, threw it over the horns and eyes of the infuriated beast and, darting by its side, drove the arrow or the lance into its heart. Others suddenly dashed off on the prairie by the side of the affrighted animals which had escaped and, closely escorting them for a few *rods*, brought down their *carcasses* upon the turf.

This picture is from a painting by George Catlin, an artist who travelled across the plains in the early 1830s. It shows one of the ways the Indians killed the buffalo. It was called 'running the buffalo'. Can you guess why a long leather strap trailed from the horse's neck?

Yet a third way of catching buffalo was for the tribe to go *downwind* of a herd and then stampede it either into a *box canyon*, or into a strong pen, or over steep cliffs like those in the Yellowstone Valley.

The dead animals were then butchered by the women. After a hard winter the whole tribe stood around waiting to eat the raw livers and tongues as they were cut from the carcasses. These meats were packed with vitamins, something the Indians lacked in their winter meals. The women peeled back the skins and cut out the meats. Then they removed the stomachs, intestines and sinews, and sawed off the bones, including the horns and hooves. Finally, everything was wrapped in the skins and carried back to the camp. Then the roasting fires were lit and the meat racks and spits made ready for the feasting and rejoicing. Rib steaks soon began to sizzle, while pieces of liver, 23 lights, sweetbreads, kidneys and tongues began to cook in the buffalo pouches hung from wooden tripods over the fire. The pouches contained water as well as the meats and the contents were boiled by heating stones in the fire and then dropping them into the water inside the pouches.

In the days following, the women were very busy. The meat was sliced into long strips and dried on racks over the fire. Once dry, the meat was pounded hard and flavoured with crushed berries. Melted fat and marrow were then poured over the mixture. Finally the meat was rolled up and packed away in leather bags until needed.

The women also had the laborious job of preparing the hides and robes from the buffalo skins. Each skin was pegged down and the hair and flesh scraped off with tools made from stone, elkhorn or buffalo bone. Afterwards, every day the women sprinkled the hides with a *tanning fluid* made by soaking buffalo brains in water. They then rubbed them to soften them. After about ten days the hides were soft and pliable enough to be made into light blankets, tipi covers, leggings, shirts, dresses, moccasins, knife-sheaths, *quivers*, bow cases and other leather things. To obtain robes the women did similar work but the hair was not removed and they did not smoke them, as was done with the hides. Smoking singed the hair and spoilt the look of the robes. So the skins provided winter clothing and bedding. While the women worked the men idled, resting after their hunting. They sat and smoked, talked about hunting and war, and played *lacrosse* on the open prairie.

Good hunters were important men in a Sioux tribe. Rarely did a successful hunter refuse to share his food and skins with others if they were in need. His tipi was often crowded with guests. Generosity was a Teton virtue and the children were taught it at an early age. Boys were given their first bow when they were five or six. They were taught to give away the first of each different animal they killed.

Summer, too, was the time to go to war against enemies like the Crow and Chippewas. To sneak up on an enemy camp and steal the best horses was an act which brought a warrior much

Hunting buffalo in winter

honour among his tribe. Even more honourable was to touch an enemy with one's bare hands or with a long feathered pole. Touching an enemy in this way was called 'counting coup'. It was rated even more highly than killing or scalping an enemy. Some warriors went on horse-stealing raids carrying only their feathered poles or 'coup' sticks. They would record their battle exploits by painting pictures and *symbols* on their blankets, robes and tipis. A red hand meant the warrior had been wounded by his enemy; a black hand, that he had slain his enemy. The most important place to display honours, however, was on the eagle feather worn on his head. The warrior kept several of these feathers, which were very much prized possessions. He kept his best one in a special wooden case. A red spot on the feather meant the owner had killed an enemy. Red paint round the edges of the feather, with a notch cut in it or the top clipped off, showed he had cut the throat of an enemy, and lifted his scalp.

Scalps brought back to the camp were used by women in a ceremonial Scalp Dance. Women who had lost their menfolk in battle danced with the scalps to show the tribe that their dead relatives had been revenged. First, the insides of the scalps were rubbed with blue clay or red dye and stretched over hoops fixed to long poles. Then, according to Seth Eastman, an Indian artist, who witnessed one of these ceremonies:

> The medicine men beat time on skins stretched over a *keg*, at the same time singing a monotonous *guttural* song. The *squaws* dance round the scalp in *concentric* circles. . . . After dancing five, ten, or fifteen minutes they stop and one of the squaws will state to the assembly that her father, son, brother or husband was killed by a Chippewa, or some tribe. She will conclude by saying – 'Whose scalp have I got on my shoulder?' Then a grand war whoop is given and the dance commences. The dance continues two or three months until it goes through every village of the tribe. After which the scalp is buried with a good deal of ceremony. Their richest dresses are worn in this dance.

Eastman also described another dance which the Sioux felt was very important. This was the Dog Dance and it was performed by warriors to show visitors to the camp how brave they were in battle and how they would eat out the hearts of their enemies.

> The Sioux warriors formed a circle; in the centre was a pole fastened to the ground. One of the Indians killed a dog, and, taking out the heart and liver, held them for a few moments in a bucket of cold water, and then hung them to the pole. After a while, one of the warriors advanced towards it barking . . . he tried to make himself look as much as possible like a dog. He retreated, and another warrior advanced with a different sort of bark; more joined in, until there

Left: *This is a painting of Indians travelling. It was painted by Seth Eastman who lived in the west and observed the Indians closely. Notice how detailed the painting is. Can you see how the woman is carrying the child on her back?*

was a chorus of barking. Next, one becomes very courageous, jumps and barks towards the pole, biting off a piece of flesh; another follows and does the same *feat*. One after another they all bark and bite.

The warriors could end up pale and sick after this dance.

The most important tribal ceremony of the year was the Sun Dance. The highlight of this dance was when volunteers thrust skewers through their chests and attached them by long strings to the top of a large pole. Then they danced round the pole, eating and drinking nothing, and praying and looking towards the sun at all times. This self-torture demonstrated to the tribe the dancer's bravery. It also brought on *hallucinations*, dreaming, or 'visions', in which the dancer made contact with the spirit world. The dancer hoped the spirits would then make him a better hunter or warrior and bring good fortune to the tribe.

The Teton believed in a Sky Father who watched over the world, protected the Indians, and governed the animals. Like the Nez Percé he thought that spirits were everywhere around him in nature. It was very important for him to please the spirits because then they would make him brave in hunting and war, generous to his friends, and faithful to his family and tribe. Only by being those things would he win the tribe's respect and, perhaps, be chosen as one of its leaders.

A medicine man, therefore, was a very important person to the Sioux Indians. They believed he had 'magic' powers because he could talk to the spirits, learn their thoughts and feelings, and even persuade them to do what he asked. Before a hunt or battle the medicine man was asked to find out if the spirits were on the tribe's side. If he said they were not, the hunt or war might be called off until the medicine man had won them over. When people fell ill, he was called in to make them well. Healing powers were part of the medicine man's magic.

The medicine man, however, was not left to contact the spirits all by himself. The hunter believed that when he killed an animal its soul went to the spirit world. There it told the spirits how its body had been killed, cut up and used. There was a proper way to do these things. After each buffalo hunt, for example, the tribe always left the best-dressed buffalo robe on the plains. It was a gift to Tatanka, the buffalo god, for his help in catching the animals.

Boys and youths learned these proper ways of hunting from their uncles or friends of their fathers, and from the animal spirits themselves. When his elders thought it was time, the young Sioux was taken out into the plains and left to sit alone, perhaps for days, without food or drink. He had to pray for a dream or 'vision' in which an animal would tell him how to hunt properly. The medicine men of the tribe would tell the youth what his dream meant. The animal in the vision became the hunter's guardian spirit and he kept a *memento* of it as the Nez Percé did. His adult name might be Red Deer or Running Deer. While young, a boy or girl had names like 'long ears', 'big nose', 'flat head', or 'without teeth'. Such silly names were thought to act as a spur to children to learn their tasks properly. Then they received respectable names like the ones just mentioned. If no animal appeared in the vision, the Teton would take gifts to a medicine man who would give him a guardian spirit and a memento. No Indian was ever without one. It was one of his sacred possessions.

4 The Coming of the Americans

This is a painting of Lewis and Clark. Between 1804 and 1806 they led the first American military expedition west of the River Missouri and crossed the hunting grounds of the Sioux and the Nez Percés

In 1800 the great Mississippi river marked the western boundary of the USA. Only a very small number of Americans had ever crossed it. During the next sixty years they poured across the plains, mountains and deserts as far as the Pacific coast. First came small military expeditions and small groups of fur traders and trappers, numbering a few hundred men. But later, in the 1840s and 1850s, came the settlers and the miners.

Quickly their numbers swelled to many thousands as their wagon trains headed west to California, Oregon and Texas. In making these journeys the Americans came face to face with the wild Indians, including the Apaches, the Sioux and the Nez Percés.

By 1848 the USA, by purchase, bargaining and war, had gained nearly all the land between the Mississippi and the Pacific. The homelands of the Apaches, Sioux and Nez Percés were thus brought within the boundaries of the USA. The Indians, of course, at that time were unaware of these changes. Map 5 shows the expansion of the American nation between 1800 and 1848. Map 6 will help you to follow the events mentioned in the rest of this chapter.

At first, the meetings between the Americans and the Indians were usually friendly. As the fur trade developed on the plains and the western mountains the Indians sold more and more furs to trading companies like the Rocky Mountain Fur Company. The Nez Percés, for example, were frequent visitors to the mountain meeting place of the trappers.

The Nez Percés, too, showed interest in the white man's religion, and in 1836 they invited a missionary, the Reverend Henry Spalding, and his family to live among them. A Christian mission was built at Lapwai and there Spalding taught the Nez Percés about Jesus and the Bible, how to read and write, and how to grow crops and rear cattle. Some Nez Percés changed their whole way of life. They stopped going to the buffalo country and settled down as farmers.

Meanwhile, on the plains, trading posts were built at Fort Laramie, Fort Union, Fort McKenzie and Pierre. Here the Indians began to take their furs and skins to trade for guns, food, blankets, trinkets and whisky. Prizing the white man's goods the Indians increased their trade at the forts. After the hunting seasons their tipis were pitched outside the walls of the forts. At Fort Laramie, on the trail to California and Oregon, the Indians even gathered to trade with the people of the wagon trains. Many tipis remained at this fort all the year round. The fur trade was very important to the Teton Sioux.

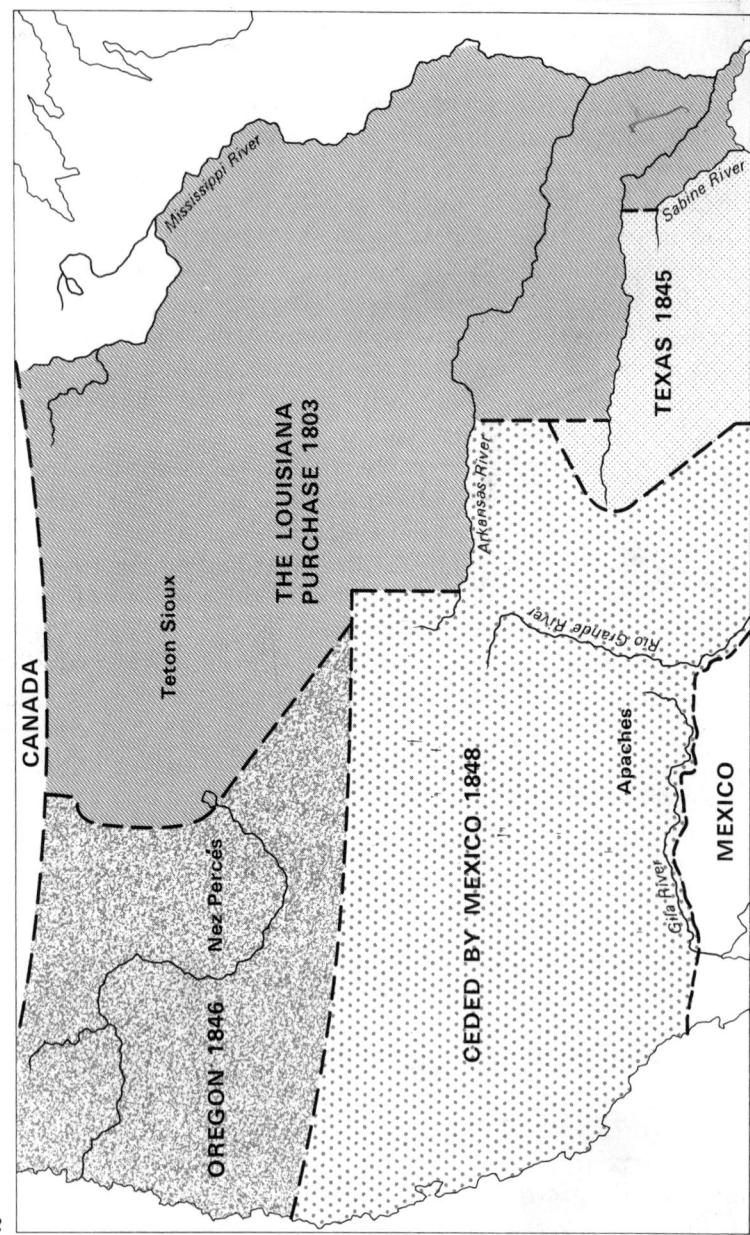

MAP 5   This map shows how, in the years 1803–1848, the white Americans were aquiring more and more land, much of which contained the hunting grounds of the Sioux, the Apaches and the Nez Percés

CANADA

Mississippi River

Teton Sioux

THE LOUISIANA
PURCHASE 1803

Sabine River

TEXAS 1845

Arkansas River

Rio Grande River

OREGON 1846

Nez Percés

CEDED BY MEXICO 1848

Apaches

Gila River

MEXICO

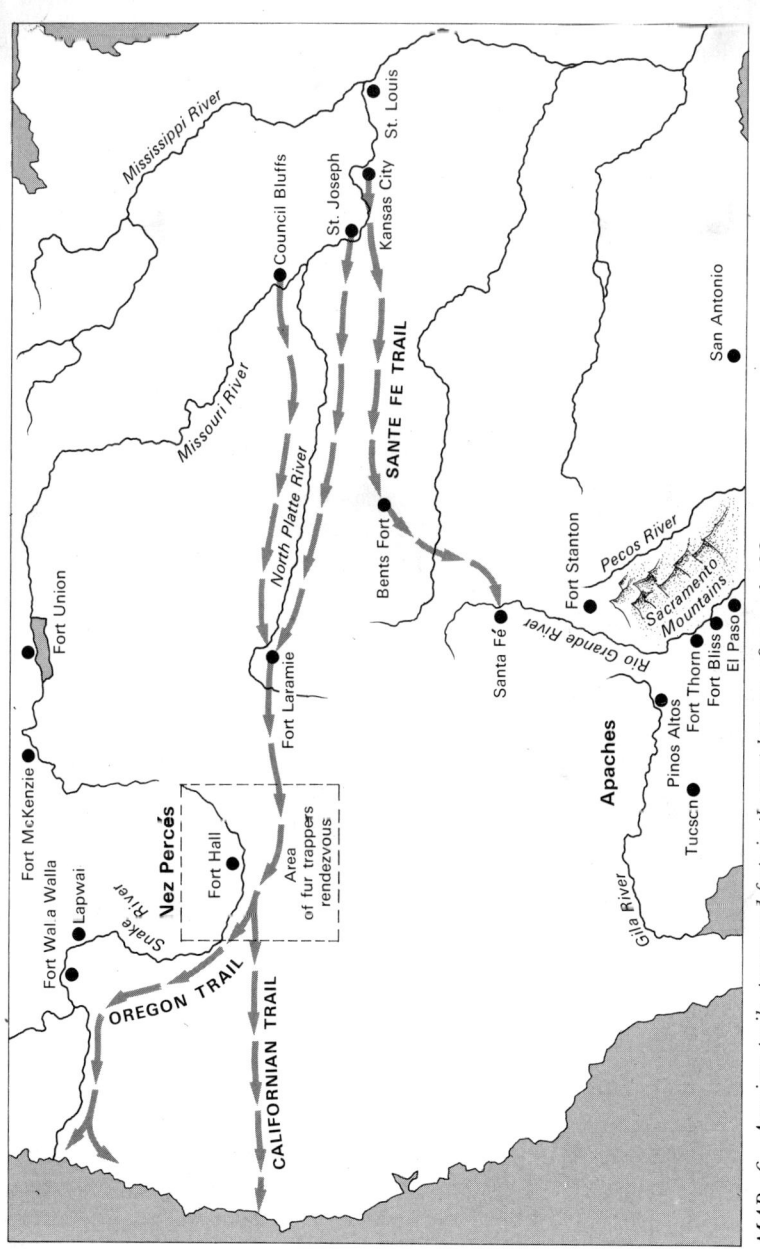

MAP 6 American trails, towns and forts in the west between 1800 and 1860

Indians arriving to trade at Fort Laramie. Notice how easy it was for the Americans to defend the fort

Far away, in the south-west, even some of the Apaches tried to be friendly to the Americans. As the white settlers filled up the plains and valleys of Texas the Apaches found themselves with less room to hunt. Their food supplies grew scarcer. Across the Rio Grande, in Mexico, they were very unwelcome. Indeed, as we have seen, the Mexican government was trying to wipe out the Apaches. The scalp hunters were busy for a while after

1837. Many Jicarilla and Mescalero Apaches therefore believed it best to make peace with the Americans. They knew they stood little chance in a war against them. In 1850 these tribes, with the Comanche Indians, asked for peace talks with the Governor of New Mexico. A year later a treaty was signed. The Governor hoped to place these Indians on land remote from American settlers so that both sides could live in peace. Unfortunately, he did not have enough money to make his ideas work.

Both the Americans and the Indians had their men of peace – people who wanted their side to be trusting and friendly towards the other. But this was not to be. On both sides, too, there were men who lied, cheated, robbed and killed. Quarrelling and fighting occurred between the Americans and the Indians. Fears, suspicions and hatreds were born. Each side swore revenge on the other and was careless about the people it accused and killed. Peaceful Indians were murdered along with the war-like ones. Innocent Americans were raided as much as the guilty ones. Let us give some examples of all this.

As the fur trade on the plains grew, the Sioux came to live and hunt between the Platte River and the Black Hills. They traded more and more at the American forts. A favourite trick of the traders was to give whisky to the Indians, get them drunk, and then either offer very little against the furs or even take the furs for nothing. Some Sioux were killed or murdered. Others died from diseases like smallpox or measles that they caught from the whites. Light Haired Boy, who later became Crazy Horse, the great Oglala war chief, sometimes visited Fort Laramie with his father. He never forgot how badly the Oglalas were treated by the Americans. He always remembered his own father angrily calling on the tribe to drive out the white man before it was too late.

Settlers and miners angered the Sioux when they sent out men from their wagon trains to hunt the buffalo that was so important to the Sioux. Sioux war parties hit back by running off horses, mules and cattle, and attacking wagons which fell behind the main body of the wagon train.

One happening was long remembered by the Sioux. In 1854 a cow got loose from a wagon train and ran into an Indian camp. Its owner, too scared to go after it, told the soldiers at Fort Laramie that the Indians had stolen it. Conquering Bear, the chief of the Sioux Camp, offered to pay for the cow but the soldiers opened fire on the village. Fierce fighting took place. All the soldiers were killed. Conquering Bear was mortally wounded. Frightened that more soldiers would come, the Oglalas moved away deep into the plains, away from the wagon trains and forts.

A few days after this battle Light Haired Boy had a vision. He saw a rider with long brown hair coming towards him. The horseman wore no war paint. He had a small smooth stone behind his ear. As he rode bullets and arrows were fired at him but he was not hurt. Indians tried to hold him back but failed. Then a thunderstorm began. On the rider's cheek Light Haired Boy saw a mark like zigzag lightning. Hailspots glistened on his body and a small red-backed hawk flew over his head.

For a long time Light Haired Boy kept the vision a secret. When he was sixteen he told his father, who was a medicine man, about his vision. His father explained its meaning to him. He must trust his vision. He must lead his people against their enemies. If he was unafraid he would not be killed by bullets or arrows. In battle he must wear a small brown stone and hawk feathers. He must paint the symbol of lightning on his cheek and hailspots on his body.

Meanwhile, each year in Oregon, white settlers were reaching the end of the trial, looking round for the best land and starting their farms and ranches. In the early years very few settled on Nez Percé land although farms did appear at the Dalles, a favourite trading place of the Indians. Many Nez Percés began to suspect the Reverend Spalding of sending for white men. In 1848, fearing for his life, Spalding fled from the Nez Percé country. Other whites stayed on. Some became horse dealers. Their trade sometimes was built up on animals stolen from the Nez Percés.

We have said already that some Apache tribes tried to make

This engraving shows how the Indians avoided being hit by the bullets of their enemies

peace with the Americans. This was the case with the Jicarillas. But just after the treaty was made some soldiers had fired at these Indians. They had no reason to open fire. The Jicarillas were so angry that they began to attack wagon trains and stagecoaches in the west of Texas. Some Americans were killed. Others formed a *posse*, chased the Indians and killed seven of them. The Apaches killed a woman and child whom they had captured. That night, in camp the Americans heard a noise nearby. Later one of them wrote:

> At first we supposed it to be an animal of some kind. Three or four of us made an examination through the willow bushes and found an Indian child which I suppose was

37

about eight months old. It was strapped to a board. An old gruff soldier stepped up and said; 'Let me see that brat.' I handed it to him. He picked up a heavy stone, tied it to the board, dashed baby and all into the water, and in a moment no trace of it was left. The soldier's only comment was, 'You're a little feller now but will make a big Injun bye and bye. I only wish I had more to treat the same way.'

It did not take long for the American settlers and miners to demand their government's protection from the hostile Indians. The American government was put in a difficult position. In earlier years it had believed that the great plains of the Louisiana Purchase were fit only for the Indians to live there. In 1834 the *Federal government* had told the Indians that this land was theirs 'as long as the stars shall shine and rivers flow'. Within twenty years this promise was broken.

In 1849 the American government bought Fort Laramie from the American Fur Company. Soldiers were sent to garrison it and to protect the wagon trains on the California and Oregon Trails. In the same year Fort Bliss was established near the Rio Grande to protect the wagon trains and stage coaches passing between Texas and New Mexico. In the next few years several other forts were built along the Rio Grande in an effort to stop Apache raiding. Far north, in Oregon, Fort Walla Walla was built near the end of the Oregon Trail to give support to the whites as they set up their farms.

The forts were not there simply to defend the *emigrants*. The Federal government knew that soon *transcontinental* railroads would be built across the plains and mountains to the Pacific Coast. The Platte Valley was one likely route to the Far West. Another was through El Paso, in Apache country. In the early 1850s railroad surveyors were in Nez Percé country looking for a northern route to the west coast. The Indians would have to be kept away from these very important lines of communication.

In 1851 the government asked Thomas Fitzpatrick, a famous
mountainman and fur trader, to call the Indians of the central

plains to a great council at Fort Laramie. To the Indians Fitzpatrick was called Broken Hand. They trusted and respected both him and Jim Bridger, another great mountainman, who acted as an interpreter. Between eight and twelve thousand Indians rode to the Fort Laramie council. Their tipis covered the plains for miles on every side of the fort. The American officials made speeches and gave away many blankets, beads, mirrors and food. They asked the Indians to allow the wagon trains to pass safely. They wanted each Indian nation to keep within a certain area of land.

The Sioux were part of the large gathering at Fort Laramie. Like the other Indians they accepted the gifts and listened to the speeches. The Americans chose a Brulé Sioux chief, Conquering Bear, to be the head chief of the entire Sioux nation. (He died in 1854 near Fort Laramie in the incident described on page 36.) He promised that the Sioux would keep to the lands of Dakota, north of the River Platte. In return, the American government guaranteed to pay the Sioux large sums of money each year as long as they kept their promise. The whites, however, did not seem to understand that no one person could speak for the whole Sioux nation. No one chief could promise to keep it within a certain area. The Sioux nation was made up of many tribes, each with its own leaders.

Four years later a similar council was held at Fort Walla Walla. To this meeting were invited many of the coastal and mountain Indian tribes of Oregon. About 5,000 warriors attended, many with their wives and children. On the opening day of the meeting:

> A thousand Nez Percé warriors rode in, two abreast, naked to the waist, their face painted with white, yellow and red paint in fanciful designs and decked with plumes and feathers and trinkets fluttering in the sunshine. Before the American peace commissioners they charged at full gallop, firing their guns, brandishing their shields, beating their drums, and yelling their war whoops.

The Americans said they wanted to give the Oregon Indians

teachers, money, tools and equipment so that they could become weavers and spinners, farmers and mechanics, and doctors and lawyers. In return, the Indians must settle down on reservations and give up part of their hunting grounds.

The Nez Percés were the hardest of all the assembled Indians to deal with. Some of them, following a chief called Lawyer, were willing to accept these terms. Other Nez Percé chiefs refused them. A commotion at the council was caused when Looking Glass, a highly respected hunter and chief, returned from the buffalo country and refused to accept any reduction in the Nez Percé hunting grounds. Most Nez Percés agreed with him and the peace commissioners could not convince them otherwise.

The Apaches also proved very troublesome. Those who had wanted peace with the Americans never got it. Soldiers had fired on the Jicarillas without cause and the Indians had taken to the warpath. The Mescaleros of the Sierra Blanca (White Mountain), who sincerely wanted peace, found that often they were blamed for raids and killings which in fact had been done by Mescalero bands living further south along the Rio Grande. The raiding Mescaleros were led by a war chief called Gomez.

In 1854 the new governor of New Mexico decided to declare war on the Apaches. A full-scale invasion of the Mescalero country was made the next year, when a hundred and sixty men, cavalry and infantry, with pack animals moved to the Sacramento Mountains (see Map 6). They fought their way into the mountains and struggled upwards to the main encampment of the Indians at about 2,700 metres. Snow and ice were everywhere. Animals became exhausted and died. The grave of one soldier was later found torn open. Wolves had half-eaten the body and ravens and turkey-buzzards had picked out the eyes and the flesh off the bones. The Indians, however, were severely beaten. The soldiers drove them from their tipis and into the wilderness without food or shelter. Many Mescaleros were killed. The rest went to Fort Thorn to ask for peace.

The outcome was the creation of the Mescalero reservation
at Fort Stanton. At first, the government gave the Mescaleros

This engraving shows an Indian about to attack an American Wagon. Notice the way he makes use of the rock to protect himself

no help at all. The Indians starved. They stole food from the whites. They ran back to the Sierra Blanca. But in November of 1856 the Mescaleros were given blankets, shirts, knives, tobacco and food and told that these things would be given to them each month as long as they behaved themselves. The land was planted with corn and vegetables and the Mescaleros began to farm their reservation. Except for the years 1861 to 1872, for reasons we shall see soon, the Fort Stanton reservation has been the Mescalero home ever since.

5 Cochise, Victorio, Geronimo and the Hostile Apaches

The Apaches were the hardest of all the wild Indians for the Americans to defeat. They lived high in their mountain strongholds. They moved through the wilderness at an amazing speed. They made sudden and surprise attacks on their enemies. When pursued, they retreated into the mountains and deserts and seemed to vanish. The Apaches, too, had many brave and intelligent leaders. Mangas Coloradas, Cochise and Victorio were all chiefs of their tribes. Others, like Geronimo, were fierce and resourceful men whose war parties made many successful raids on the whites. The wars between the Apaches and the Americans lasted for more than thirty years, ending finally in 1886 when Geronimo surrendered.

We have seen already that the Mescaleros, Jicarillas and Mimbrenos, made war against the Americans almost from the time the whites entered their territory (see maps 2 and 5), and that the Mescaleros were defeated in 1855 and forced to live on a reservation.

The Indians, however, were unhappy on the reservation. White men sold them whisky and several times settlers around Fort Stanton attacked and killed them. Then, in 1861, the American Civil War began. Fort Stanton became deserted. The Mescaleros saw their chance. They went back to the mountains and the warriors resumed their raids on the roads, farms and settlements in the valleys of the Rio Grande and Pecos rivers.

To the west, along the Gila River, the Mimbreno Apaches under Mangas Coloradas continued to fight the Americans. In 1861 they were joined on the warpath by the Chiricahuas, led by Cochise, who had for ten years kept the peace with the Americans. Stage coaches carrying passengers and mail between El Paso and California, for example, had passed unharmed through the Dragoon Mountains, the Chiricahua home. Indeed, the warriors of Cochise even supplied wood for a stage station they allowed to be built in Apache Pass.

In 1860, however, a small band of hostile Apaches had raided a white man's ranch, kidnapped a small boy, and stolen some cattle. The settler believed the Apaches were Chiricahuas. A detachment of soldiers went to Apache Pass to meet Cochise who rode down from the mountains to greet them. The army lieutenant, who knew nothing about Cochise or Indians, accused the Apache chief of the raid. Cochise said he had not done it and became angry when the lieutenant said he was lying. The chief was known always to speak honestly and truthfully. Drawing his knife Cochise slashed open the side of the tent in which he had been talking to the officer. He leapt past the startled guards surrounding the tent, and escaped up the hillside. Afterwards, the Apaches referred to this escape as 'Cut Through the Tent'.

The next day a wagon train was destroyed. Two men were burned alive and two held prisoner. The stage coach from Tucson was ambushed and the stage station in Apache Pass attacked. The army lieutenant moved his men to the station and sent for reinforcements.

Cochise then rode within shouting distance of the station and asked the soldiers to release his brother and two nephews captured during his talk with them. The lieutenant refused, saying that Cochise must first return the boy and the cattle. Again, the Indian said he was not to blame. The next day Cochise again tried to talk but the lieutenant would not change his mind. Very angry now, Cochise dragged one of his American prisoners to death behind his running horse. Later he put two more captives to death as well. In retaliation the soldiers hung six Apaches from an oak tree. Among them were the brother and nephew of Cochise. He said that for every Apache killed his warriors would kill ten whites.

An engraving by Remington showing Apaches ambushing a cavalryman who was on watch

The ten years from 1861 were a time of cruel, savage and bloody warfare. Cochise terrorised Arizona. Whites were burned at the stake, hung upside down over fires and skinned alive, or tied down over anthills, their faces smeared with honey.

The Americans were just as bloodthirsty. In 1864 the soldiers, with the help of some miners, captured Mangas Coloradas. The same night, acting under army orders, the two soldiers guarding the sleeping chief burned his feet and legs with bayonets heated in the fire. Then the soldiers shot him dead. The army report noted that the Indian was 'killed while attempting to escape'. His head was cut off and sent to Washington.

Meanwhile, further east, another war against the Mescaleros was starting. Kit Carson, the famous mountainman, was given command of some troops, told to re-occupy Fort Stanton, and then wipe out the Indians. His orders said:

> All Indian men of that tribe are to be killed whenever and wherever you can find them. The women and children will not be harmed, but you will take them prisoner, and feed them at Fort Stanton. You have no power to make peace; If they beg for peace, their chiefs and twenty of their principal men must come to Santa Fé to have a talk there.

Once again American troops marched into the Sacramentos. At Dog Canyon they surprised five hundred Mescaleros and killed many of them. Those that escaped went straight to Kit Carson at Fort Stanton and surrendered. Cadete, their chief, said:

> 'You are stronger than we, We have fought you as long as we had rifles and powder; but your weapons are better than ours. Give us like weapons and turn us loose, we will fight you again; but we are worn out; we have no more heart; we have no provisions, and no means to live; your troops are everywhere; you have driven us from our last and best stronghold and we have no more heart. Do with us as may seem good to you, but do not forget that we are men and braves.'

The Mescaleros, however, could not stay at Fort Stanton. They were sent to a new reservation, the Bosque Redondo, where they had to do exactly what they were told. Within a year most Mescaleros had deserted it.

Life on the new reservation was unendurable. Unusually bad weather, diseases of crops and people, scarcity of fuel, foul drinking water, diseased meat rations, and trouble with the Navaho Indians also sent to live there – these things were more than the Mescaleros could stand. Some of them joined with Cochise while others rode to their cousins in the Davis and Guadalupe Mountains. From there they resumed their raids along the Rio Grande and Pecos valleys.

Other Apaches who gave in to the soldiers also received harsh treatment. In 1871, for example, several hundreds had surrendered to the soldiers at Camp Grant. Yet the citizens of Tucson said they were a menace. One day, at dawn, men from Tucson attacked the Apache camp, killing ten men and a hundred and eight women and children. Twenty-seven children, captured alive were sold into slavery. Such behaviour not only enraged the Apaches still on the warpath but also shocked many Americans.

By this time the total cost of the wars against the Apaches was over forty million dollars. Despite this, the Indians were far from being defeated· The Americans now changed their policy. Instead of trying to wipe out the Apache warriors they sent an *envoy* to talk peace with the Indians and persuade them to settle down peacefully on land reserved for them away from the white settlements. This policy of peace seemed promising. The 1870s were a much quieter decade than the 1860s.

Settling a peace with Cochise was not easy. Growing old, he knew he could not fight much longer. Nevertheless, he kept his Chiricahuas on the warpath until the Americans agreed to his terms. His reservation must be in the Dragoon Mountains. The American *agent* at the reservation must be Tom Jeffords, his close friend and the one white man he trusted fully. In 1872 the Americans finally agreed and Cochise lived peacefully on his reservation until his death in 1874. The old chief was buried in his beloved mountains. No one knows exactly where his grave is. All night long horses were ridden over the burial place until all traces of it were gone. The only white man who knew was Tom Jeffords and he kept the secret until he died.

Other reservations were established too. In 1872 one was opened at San Carlos. Amongst the Apaches who settled there were some Mimbrenos and Chiricahuas. Most Mimbrenos, however, settled at Ojo Caliente (Warm Springs) in a valley called Canada Alamosa. The Mescaleros were given back their reservation at Fort Stanton. Map 7 shows all these places.

This policy of dispersing the Apaches on several reservations lasted only until 1876. Then the American government decided to place all the Apaches west of the Rio Grande on one reservation at San Carlos. It was too expensive to run several reservations and the white settlers were pressing the government for more land, too. First the Chiricahuas and then the Mimbrenos were moved.

San Carlos was hated by the Apaches. Kaywaykla, whom we have mentioned already, was told by his grandmother that San Carlos was:

'a place of death. Few people can endure a summer there. Before you were born I went to that terrible place. There was nothing but cactus, rattlesnakes, heat, rocks and insects. No game; no *edible* plants. Many, many of our people died of starvation.'

An American army officer who was garrisoned there called it 'Hell's Forty Acres'. Centipedes, rattlers and poisonous spiders were found in the soldiers' bedding. Apaches died from *malaria* during the long hot summer.

Victorio, chief of the Warm Springs Apaches, decided to lead his people from San Carlos back to the Ojo Caliente. Arriving back there Victorio tried hard to persuade the Americans to let his people remain at Warm Springs, among the streams, forests and mountains they loved. His pleas fell on deaf ears. In 1879 Victorio was told to take his people back to San Carlos. Some of the Warm Springs Apaches agreed to return. They were led by a man called Loco. Victorio was not willing to go back. Nor was Nana, an old Apache fighter highly respected by his people. Both agreed to fight the white man. About forty warriors and some women and children 47

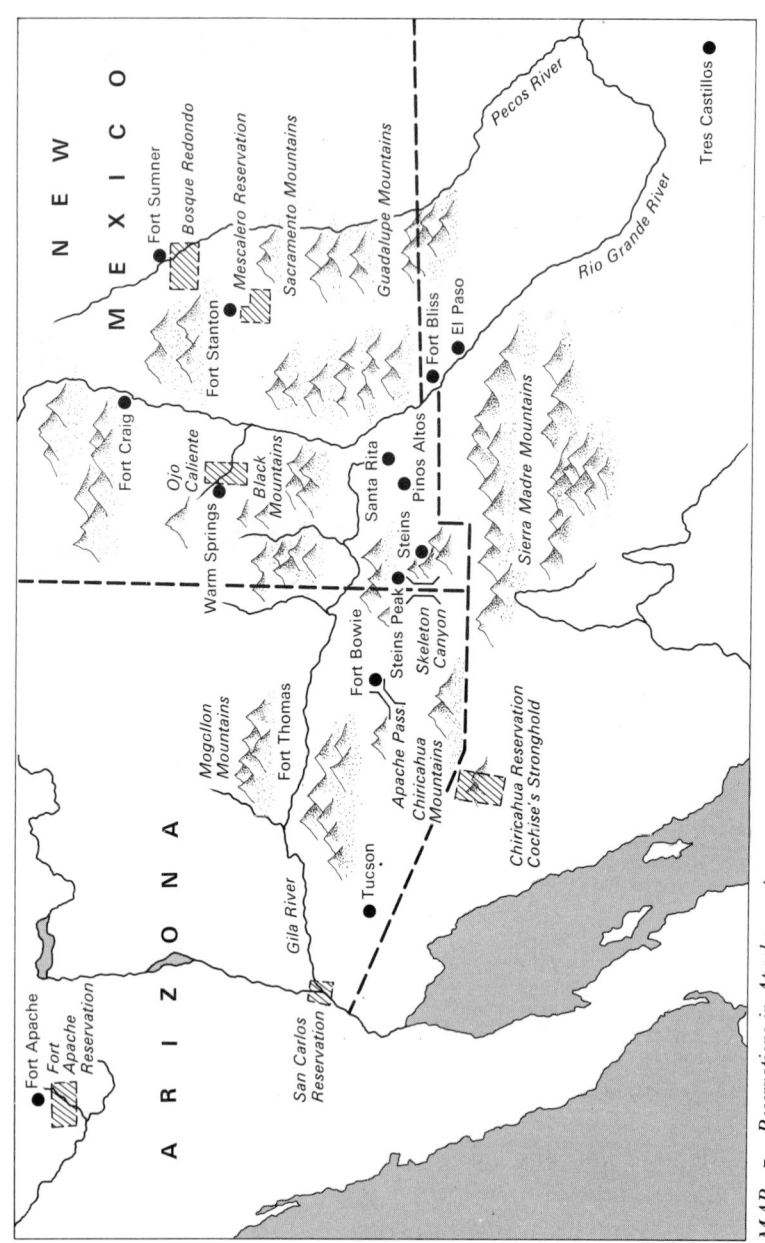

MAP 7   Reservations in Apache country

This is a model in an American Museum showing how the Apaches lived on a reservation. Notice the baby's cradle and the wicker jug being coated with pitch to make it waterproof

decided to go with Victorio and Nana. This war party left the reservation in 1879. Most of the people in it never returned.

Months before this departure Victorio and Nana had been preparing for war. They had led or sent out parties of warriors to raid the surrounding areas. Guns, ammunition, blankets and food were stolen from soldiers, ranchers and miners, and from Mexicans in Sonora. These goods were hidden in *caches* scattered along the mountain trails between the Ojo Caliente and Mexico. These caches played a very important part in Apache warfare against the soldiers. Try to think why. In Mexico itself Victorio remained friendly with the sheep-herders and farmers. As long as they gave him food, guns and ammunition his warriors left them in peace. If they refused they were killed.

Then came the retreat into Mexico. Kaywaykla wrote:

49

For weeks we fled from one range to another, crossing the open plains at night, with a strong advance guard preceding the women and children and warriors bringing up the rear. . . . Children rode behind grandmothers or in *tsachs* until the aged were forced to drop out and be left in secret retreats. If there were new babies sometimes these and their mothers were left. But the great majority kept on, with little food, with no fires, and often with terrible weakness and fatigue, but without complaint. I doubt that any people ever excelled us as mountain climbers. Scaling walls was taken for granted. When closely pursued we killed our horses and scaled cliffs no enemy could climb. Men tied ropes to women and children and lifted them from ledge to ledge until they could take cover or escape. If the women and children could go ahead the warriors picked off the scouts, who always preceded the cavalry. We moved at night only when forced to do so and never fought in the darkness unless attacked. There was a belief that he who kills at night must walk in darkness through the Place of the Dead.

For the next two years Victorio and his warriors raided and killed in Arizona, Texas and New Mexico and south of the border in Mexico. Both American and Mexican armies chased him yet they could never catch him. In his campaigns, a hundred soldiers and four hundred civilians were killed. Then, in October, 1880 when Victorio had retreated into Mexico, he was seen, by chance, in a canyon near the Tres Castillos Mountains. He was travelling there to wait for the return of a raiding party sent out to capture ammunition. The Mexican soldiers closed in and in the fierce fighting Victorio was killed.

The death of Victorio was a serious blow to the Apaches on the warpath. But they were not finished yet. Nana, now about seventy years old, wrinkled and aching with rheumatism, continued to fight against the whites. Kaywaykla said of him:

Nana, deeply and sincerely wanted peace, but he wanted his own country, his freedom, and that of his people to enjoy living in their own land. Aged and infirm [weak], he fought for people, land and freedom to the inevitable, tragic end. If he were ill or weary, only he knew it. His endurance seemed endless, his patience effortless. No young man in the tribe could spend more hours in the saddle without rest than he. I am sure Mother realised that he was often weary and discouraged, but she did not speak of it in my presence. He continued to set the pace for the young men, always taking upon himself whatever hazards [dangers] had to be met.

In July and August of 1881 he and forty warriors rode over 1,500 kilometres, raiding deep into New Mexico. He fought and won eight battles, killed at least thirty whites and stole two hundred horses and mules. He was chased by a thousand soldiers and hundreds of civilians but he vanished back to Mexico. Four of his warriors were hurt but everyone in his war party got back to Mexico alive.

Geronimo, Chihuahua, Nana, Chief Loco and Ulzana. Five of the greatest leaders of the Apaches dressed in white man's clothes

About this time a band of Chiricahuas, led by Geronimo, left San Carlos. Geronimo was not an Apache war chief. The Chiricahuas as a whole refused to accept him. Some thirty or forty of their warriors, however, took him as their leader and Geronimo quickly became an Apache name feared by all whites.

With Geronimo on the warpath the Apache wars were not over. General Crook was recalled to Arizona in 1882. (Crook had helped to persuade the Apaches to settle on reservations in 1874 and 1875.) His task was to end the Apache troubles once and for all. Crook knew more than any white man about Indians. He talked and listened to the complaints of the Apaches still on the reservation. He stopped the robbing and cheating of the Indians by the agents and traders. The daily roll call of names at the agency building was ended. Instead, each Apache band was given a letter and every warrior a number. Each man was issued with a brass tag on which was stamped his letter and a number. So when Indians were reported absent from the reservation, a roll call could be ordered and the missing people named. The women and children were not tagged since they never left San Carlos without their menfolk. In 1883 the Apaches were allowed to live where they liked on the reservation. Previously they had been made to live close to the agency buildings. Horse harnesses, wagons, ploughs and bags of corn and wheat seed were issued, and the Indians were told to work at becoming farmers.

While all these changes were being made at San Carlos, Crook also made plans to hunt down the hostile Apaches led by Geronimo and Nana in Mexico. Believing that it took an Indian to catch an Indian, he increased the number of Apache scouts (recruited from among the peaceful Indians on the reservation) under his command. Crook also made up five pack trains of mules to carry the soldiers' food, blankets and ammunition. Each train had forty mules, a chief packer and ten packers. Only the fittest mules and men and the best equipment were used. With their pack trains the soldiers could now pursue the Apaches deep into the mountains and deserts, hounding

In this scene Remington shows one result of Crook's policy of setting Indian against Indian. Apaches who fled from reservations were hunted down not only by soldiers but by their own kind too

them more closely and for a much longer time.

Of great importance, too, was the agreement in 1882 between America and Mexico to permit troops of either side to cross the *international boundary* if in pursuit of Apaches on the warpath.

Crook's first expedition into Mexico was in 1883. He took two pack trains, a troop of cavalry and two hundred Apache scouts. The expedition entered the Sierra Madre early in April without being seen by Geronimo or any of the Apaches camped there. Several women and children were captured in a raid on the Apache camp. Most of the men were away raiding Mexican settlements. When the warriors returned they were stunned by the presence of American soldiers in Mexico and the capture of some of their families. So shocked were they

53

that they surrendered straight away and promised to return to San Carlos. The Apaches agreed that their families should return to the reservation with Crook's soldiers. Most of the warriors said they would come later, when they had told the other Apache camps in the Sierra Madre and when they had gathered together their animals. Crook arrived back at San Carlos in June with three hundred and twenty-five Chiricahuas and Warm Springs Indians. Fifty-two of them were warriors and they included both Nana and Loco.

Two hundred Apache warriors still remained in Mexico, including Geronimo. Slowly they journeyed back to San Carlos. Geronimo was the last to arrive. He crossed the Mexican border driving three hundred and fifty cattle stolen from Mexican ranches. But when he got to San Carlos he was forced to surrender the cattle, which were used to feed the Indians. The Mexican ranchers received money from the Americans for their stolen animals. Geronimo got nothing. This made him very angry indeed and it was one reason why he was soon to break out of the reservation again.

Indeed, the situation at San Carlos was worsening. Geronimo, Nana and several Apache sub-chiefs and warriors were unhappy on the reservation. The whites found them unwilling to help, sullen and quarrelsome. They could not forget their old way of life. To them, farming was for women. To be fair, however, it was too dry to farm without *irrigation ditches*. Crook's officers tried hard to get these dug. The newly appointed civilian agent, who wanted to be top dog, did his best to prevent them. American ranchers and merchants made profits from the sale of beef, hay and blankets to the Apaches. They did not want to see the Indians become able to look after themselves because they would lose money. Many politicians were on their side and the San Carlos agent obeyed their wishes. The Apaches were not fools. They knew the agent was against them. Before long the agent, the army and the Indians were all blaming each other for their problems. It was a situation which gave Geronimo and his supporters an excuse for breaking out from San Carlos again.

A photograph of Geronimo taken in 1886 which was the year in which he surrendered

Geronimo and Nana, with thirty-three warriors, eight youths and a hundred and one women and children, fled from San Carlos on an early May evening in 1885. The outlaws split up although most headed for Mexico. Those aiming for the border travelled the 150 kilometres without halt.

Crook now poured two thousand soldiers, five hundred Indian scouts and many pack trains into the mountains and plains of Arizona, New Mexico and Mexico. The odds were too great. One by one the Apache leaders surrendered, including Nana. Finally, only Geronimo with nineteen warriors and nineteen women and children were left. In March 1886 it all seemed over. Geronimo met Crook and surrendered to him. In the evening, however, Geronimo got drunk on *tiswin* and under cover of darkness stole away with his followers.

Crook received the blame for Geronimo's escape, yet he insisted that no one could have prevented the Indians from leaving. He resigned from his post and General Miles was put in his place. Miles sent soldiers to protect all the ranches and water holes the Apaches were likely to raid. He set up between twenty-five and thirty signalling points on the tallest mountain peaks, using *heliostat* equipment. Most of the scouts were dismissed, and cavalry and infantry sent into the mountains to track down Geronimo.

In the next few months these soldiers tracked thousands of kilometres, up and down mountainsides, in temperatures of 29°C and heavy rainfall. They surprised a number of camps and captured ponies and other equipment. The Apaches, however, re-equipped themselves by raiding Mexican ranches or the soldiers themselves. Geronimo and his warriors, hounded as they were, raided into southern Arizona, retreated to Mexico, and fought off two cavalry attacks in Sonora.

Then, in June, the soldiers captured the Indians' main camp which had much ammunition. Geronimo was told: 'Surrender, and you will be sent with your families to Florida, there to await the decision of the President as to your final disposition. Accept these terms or fight it out to the bitter end.'

Silence. . . . Geronimo then passed his hand across his eye. He asked for a drink, but it was not given. 'Take us to the reservation or fight,' replied Geronimo.

The talking went on all day, each side refusing to change their demands. The next day, after the Indians had heard that all the Chiricahuas and Warm Springs Apaches were being sent to Florida, they urged Geronimo to surrender to Miles on his terms so that they would see their families again. Geronimo agreed, and on 3 September 1886 his band handed over their weapons to General Miles who met the Indians at Skeleton Canyon on the Mexican border. The Apache wars were over.

6 Chief Joseph and the Nez Percé Retreat

In 1860 gold was found at Oro Fino Creek on the Nez Percé reservation. Very quickly a thousand miners invaded the area. Thousands more started on their way. A base depot for the miners was built at Lewiston. Then, in rapid succession, very rich strikes were made at Elk City and Florence. By January 1862, three million dollars worth of gold had been won from land on the reservation. The river valleys became busy highways to and from the goldfields. Some of the Nez Percés themselves made money from the bustling activity. They sold food and horses to the miners and acted as their guides and workers. They even ate, dressed and talked like miners. They drank the miners' whisky and got themselves into drunken brawls. The whites cheated, robbed and killed them.

Many Nez Percés, however, were angered by the presence of the miners on their land. To prevent a conflict between the Nez Percés and the miners, the American government decided to put the Indians on to a much smaller reservation than the one agreed to in 1855 at Fort Walla Walla. In 1863 the Nez Percés were called to a council meeting to agree to the new boundaries.

As before, in 1855, they were not agreed among themselves. Some, much influenced by the Christian teachings of the Reverend Spalding and again led by the same chief, Lawyer, accepted the government's proposal. They already lived in the area which the Americans wanted to be the new reservation. Other Nez Percés, however, did not. They were not willing to move and they told the *commissioner* so. But the commissioner did not listen. He wanted a treaty signed. He got

57

Lawyer to agree to the sale of about three-quarters of the Nez Percé reservation created in 1855. The price was two hundred and sixty-five thousand dollars. Lawyer, of course, had no right to sell such land. The Nez Percés had no head chief. He did not speak for all of them, only his own band. Yellow Wolf, who objected to the treaty said:

> They told us we had to give up our homes and move to another part of the reservation. That we had to give up our part of the reservation to the white people. Told us we must move in with the Nez Percés turned Christians, called upper Nez Percés by the whites. All of same tribe, but it would be hard to live together. Our religions were different, it would be hard. To leave our homes would be hard. It was these Christian Nez Percés who made with the Government a thief treaty (1863). Sold to the Government all this land. Sold what did not belong to them. We got nothing for our country. None of our chiefs signed that land-stealing treaty.

Another of the Nez Percé chiefs who rejected the 'thief' treaty was Old Joseph. He tore up his copy of it and burnt his Bible.

In 1871, just before he died, he said to his son Chief Joseph:

> Always remember that your father never sold his country. You must stop your ears whenever you are asked to sign a treaty selling your home. A few years more and white men will be all around you. They have their eyes on this land. My son, never forget my dying words. This country holds your father's body. Never sell the bones of your father and your mother.

His son, Chief Joseph, now became the leader of the Nez Percés who lived in the Wallowa Valley. The next few years were very troubled ones for him. More white settlers moved into his valley. Chief Joseph met them and explained that he did not accept the treaty of 1863. He protested strongly to the agent at Lapwai. The agent saw that Chief Joseph's claim was

Left: *Chief Joseph: the photograph was taken in the 1880s*

Below: *This engraving shows the Nez Percés attacking a wagon train in 1875. Chief Joseph could not entirely keep the peace between these Indians and the white men*

fair. He asked the government what to do. The government was not sure at first but finally said the settlers could stay in the Wallowa. Chief Joseph moved his people away from the white settlements and made another plea to the government. Meanwhile two settlers accused some Nez Percés of taking their horses. An Indian was killed. When the two whites returned they found their horses had not been stolen after all. The government, however, now tried to make Chief Joseph accept the treaty of 1863. It argued that all the Nez Percés were bound by the action of Chief Lawyer who had signed away their lands. Chief Joseph replied that:

> If we ever owned the land we own it still, for we never sold it. In the treaty councils the commissioners have claimed that our country has been sold to the government. Suppose a white man should come to me and say, 'Joseph, I like your horses, and I want to buy them'. I say to him, 'No, my horses suit me, I will not sell them.' Then he goes to my neighbour and says to him, 'Joseph has some good horses, I want to buy them but he refuses to sell.' My neighbour answers, 'Pay me the money, and I will sell you Joseph's horses.' The white man returns to me and says, 'Joseph, I have bought your horses and you must let me have them.' If we sold our lands to the government, this is the way they were bought.

Despite his arguments, Chief Joseph was told to move his people and their possessions on to the new reservation by 1 April 1877; otherwise, they would be moved by force.

The Indians did not move. Chief Joseph and other Nez Percé chiefs met with the government agent again. The order to move into the reservation was repeated. The two sides began to quarrel. Let us listen to some of it:

> 'What you talk about isn't true law at all. You white people get together, measure the earth and then divide it.'
> 'The law says "You must come to the reservation". The law is made in Washington. We don't make it.'
> 'The earth is part of my body. I never give up the earth.'

'You know very well that the government has set apart a reservation and that the Indians must go to it.'

'The Great Spirit made the world as it is and as He wanted it. And He made a part of it for us to live upon. I do not see where you get your authority to say that we shall not live where He placed us. Are you the Great Spirit? Did you make the world? Did you make the sun? Did you make the rivers run for us to drink? Did you make the grass to grow? Did you make all those things that you talk to us as though we were boys? If you did, then you have the right to talk to us as you do.'

General Howard

General Howard, who was representing the government, grew angry at this and told his soldiers to throw Tulhulhutsut, the speaker of these words, into the guardhouse. The Indians felt insulted and some were angry enough to fight. But Chief Joseph and other chiefs now agreed to talk. Within a few days they accepted lands on the reservation made under the treaty of 1863, and promised to move to them within thirty days. To his very young warriors Chief Joseph seemed a coward. He replied that 'it was better to live at peace than to begin a war and lie dead'. Chief Joseph knew that the bows and arrows of his small tribe were no match for artillery and *Gatling* guns. He knew that in a war the women and children of his tribe would 61 be killed or die of starvation, that his people would lose their horses and cattle.

Tired and discouraged, Chief Joseph's Indians moved on to Rocky Canyon where they camped with other Nez Percés to enjoy their last few days of freedom. Unfortunately, three young Nez Percés belonging to a band under White Bird, got drunk, rode out of the camp and killed four white men. Chief Joseph urged his people to keep the peace and move to the reservation. His advice was ignored. More and more Indians decided to make a fight of it, including those in Chief Joseph's band. They moved their camp deeper into the mountains and prepared for war. Chief Joseph was the last to move. When he did, he knew he must stay with his people and fight with them.

The white settlers were badly frightened by the murders of the Nez Percés already on the warpath. One of the settlers wrote a letter to General Howard, who had just returned to the area from Portland: 'We are in the midst of an Indian war. We want arms and ammunition and help at once. Don't delay a moment.'

Without waiting to hear what Chief Joseph had to say, the General sent Captain Perry with two troops of the First Cavalry from Fort Lapwai to the troubled area. At the same time he sent for reinforcements.

The Nez Percés, meanwhile, had camped in White Bird Canyon. The chiefs, including Chief Joseph, still wanted peace. They had many women and children with them. The menfolk numbered a hundred and fifty but less than half of them were able to fight.

Spoiling for a fight, the soldiers ignored the Nez Percés' *flag of truce*, shooting at the warriors who carried it. The Nez Percés now opened fire from both sides. Perry ordered his men into a long line across the slope. The volunteers went to the left, the soldiers in the centre dismounted, those to the right stayed on their horses. Suddenly, sixteen warriors charged straight at the volunteers who ran back up the slope in panic. This allowed the Indians to get behind Perry's line and attack the dismounted troopers in the centre. At the same time, a larger group of Nez Percés, led by Ollokot, or Frog, the brother of Chief Joseph, attacked on the right. The mounted soldiers fell into confusion and Perry's line was completely broken. In the centre the foot soldiers saw Indians coming at them from both sides. Within a few minutes the soldiers were cut into small groups and fighting for their lives. The warriors forced the soldiers back up the slope. Thirty-four soldiers were killed. None of the warriors was killed and they captured sixty-three rifles from their enemy.

General Howard and the whole American nation were stunned by Perry's defeat. He sent for more reinforcements, and made ready to take the field himself. He believed that Chief Joseph was his enemy, and that the Nez Percé leader was now the war chief of the hostile Indians.

With 227 troopers, twenty volunteer civilians and many packers and guides General Howard set off to defeat the hostile Indians. By the time he reached the Horseshoe Bend of the Salmon River the Nez Percés had crossed to the other side. By this time, however, the General had received news that some peaceful Nez Percés, under Chief Looking Glass, were causing trouble and likely to join the hostiles. Howard therefore split his forces and sent a detachment back to the reservation to subdue Looking Glass. He and the remaining troops crossed the river and set off after the retreating Indians, who by now had disappeared into the mountain wilderness.

For several days, in heavy rain, Howard led his men along muddy valleys and across mountain slopes. Finally, he discovered that the Nez Percés had doubled back across the Salmon at the Craig Billy Crossing. When Howard got there the Salmon River was raging so much that his men could not cross. The soldiers went back to Horseshoe Bend.

Meanwhile, a detachment of Howard's men had gone back to the reservation to deal with Looking Glass. When they arrived, all was peaceful. The news that Looking Glass was causing trouble was wrong. Indeed, as the soldiers arrived at his village, Looking Glass sent an Indian to tell them that the Nez Percés on the reservation wanted to live in peace. This message was delivered twice to the soldiers but they were in no mood to listen. A volunteer with the soldiers fired a shot and, as the peaceful Indians ran in fear for their lives, the soldiers opened fire on the camp. Then they trampled down the Nez Percé crops and rounded up the cattle and horses and drove them away. Angry and bitter, the Indians left the reservation to join the hostile Nez Percés who were moving along Cottonwood Creek from the Salmon to the South Fork of the Clearwater River.

By this time white people were very angry and disappointed with the efforts of the army under the command of General Howard. Can you think why? On the other hand, they believed that Chief Joseph had proved himself a great general and warrior. In fact, they were wrong. Chief Joseph was a man of peace. He had chosen to remain with his people in their resistance to the white man, but their fighting retreat was directed by the war chiefs – Rainbow, Five Wounds, and Ollokot.

Howard, now further reinforced, had marched four hundred soldiers and a hundred and fifty volunteers to the South Fork. From the top of some bluffs along the river he sighted the Nez Percé camp in the valley below. A four-inch howitzer and two Gatling guns were wheeled to the edge of the bluffs; they opened fire on the surprised Indians below.

Outnumbered about six to one, the hundred or so Nez Percés fought with such ferocity that Howard believed there were many more warriors than this. Shooting continued for the rest of the day. Both sides were well protected by earth, boulders and trees and few people were hit. The sun was hot and the soldiers got thirsty. There was a spring nearby but the Indians fired so well that no one could get to it. The Nez Percés drank water from the river, carried up to them by their women.

The next day saw a different story. Using the howitzer, Howard captured the spring. The soldiers started an attack on the Indian camp just afterwards. Blankets, cooking equipment and food were left behind as the Nez Percés fled down the

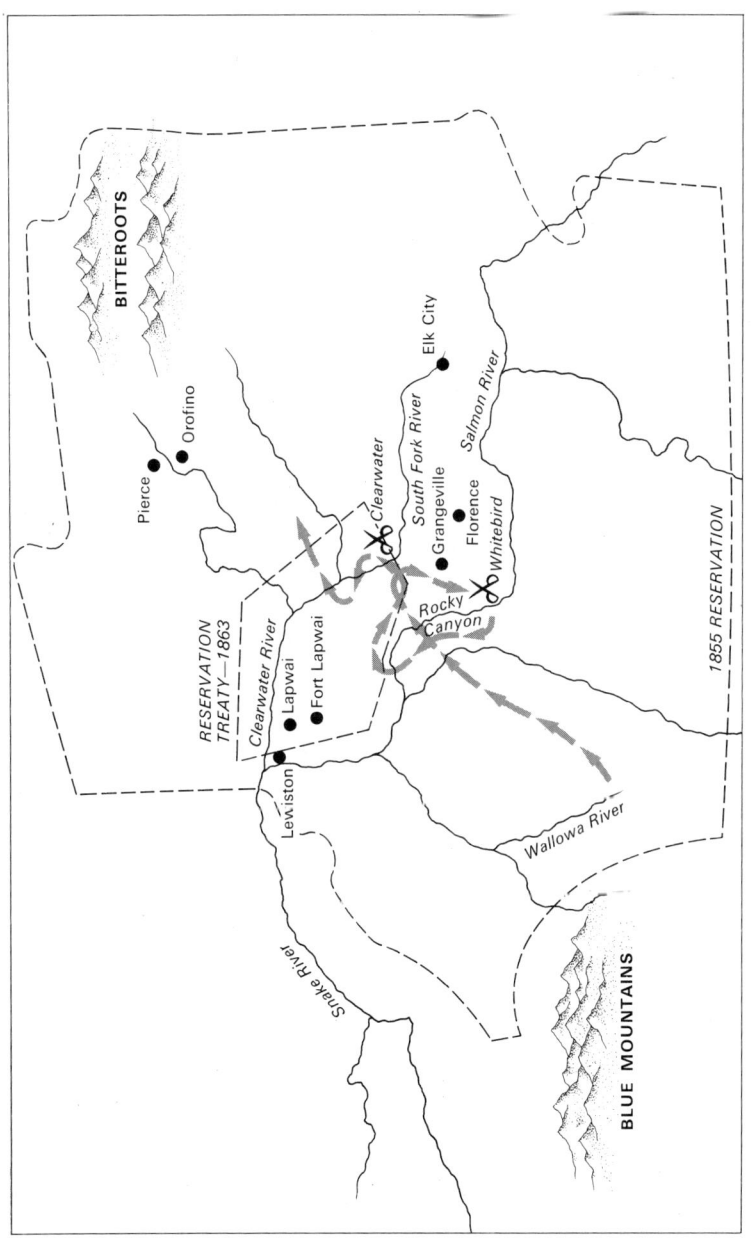

MAP 8 *The battles of Whitebird and Clearwater*

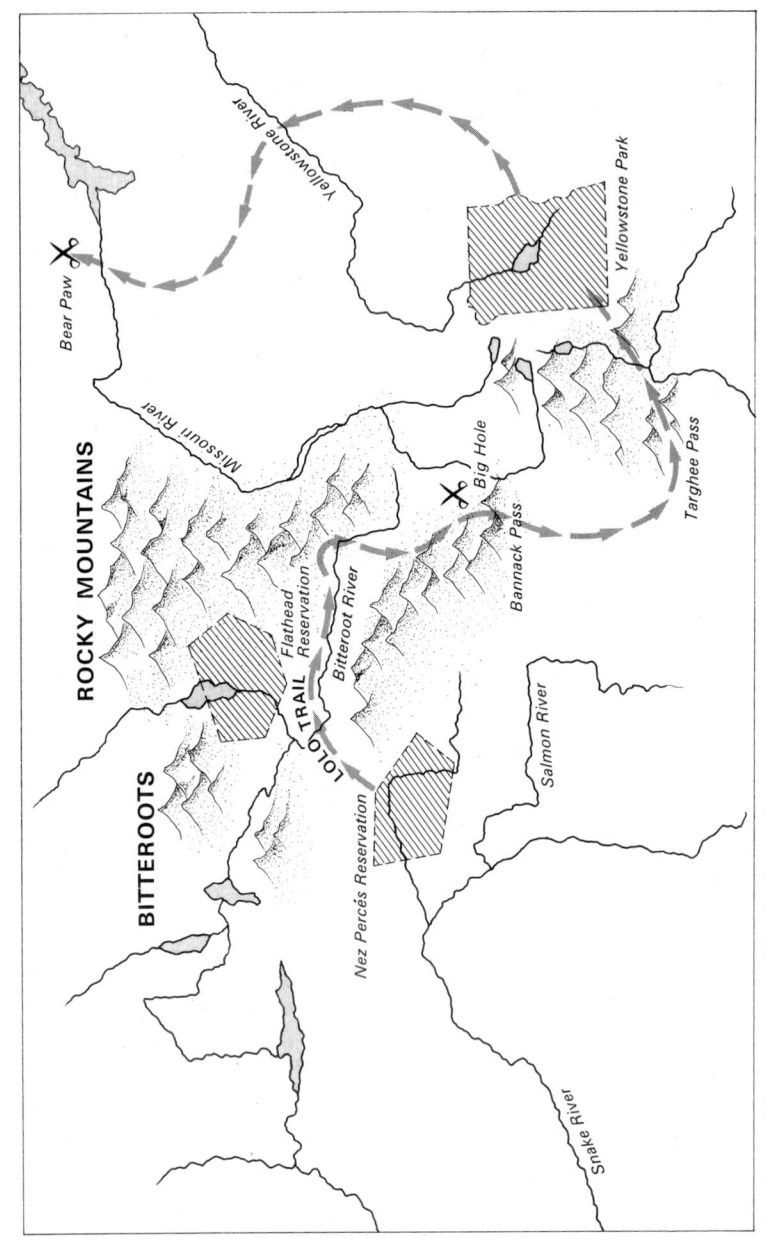

MAP 9 *The retreat of the Nez Percés in 1877*

Clearwater Valley. Howard claimed a victory, but he had lost fifteen men against four Indians. He did not pursue his enemy, however, believing he could catch up the next day. He was wrong, and his chance to end the war was lost. Map 8 shows the movements of the Nez Percés and the Battles of Whitebird and Clearwater.

Safe for the moment, the retreating Nez Percés held a council to decide what to do next. The voice of Looking Glass spoke the loudest· He said that the Nez Percés must cross the mountains to the buffalo country in Montana and hunt in peace with the Crow Indians. The Crows were buffalo hunters like the Sioux. Nez Percés had traded with them in the past. The war with the soldiers would be over. Chief Joseph and several other chiefs were reluctant to do this. It meant leaving their homeland. Yet the safety of the people was of the greatest importance and all the Nez Percés agreed to the plan of Looking Glass. He was elected the supreme war chief of the Indians for their journey to the east. Map 9 shows the route of this retreat.

The Nez Percés now took to the Lolo Trail, a thickly wooded pathway across mountainsides and along high ridges. It was a gruelling journey. They were nine days on the trail, but, at last, they emerged on the other side of the Bitterroot Mountains. At this point, some of the chiefs thought it wise to change their plans. Canada was not far away. Why not head there? Looking Glass objected: it would mean passing through the Flathead reservation and he no longer trusted these Indians. Also buffalo would be scarce. His plan to join the Crows should be kept. Again he won the argument and the Nez Percés turned south along the Bitterroot Valley. Believing themselves safe now the Nez Percés paused to rest in the Big Hole Valley. Willows lined the river, and an open meadow gave room to pitch their tipis.

But Howard had not given up. He too followed the Lolo Trail but was taking longer than the Indians. Unfortunately for the Nez Percés, another detachment of soldiers under Colonel Gibbon was moving from Fort Shaw in Montana to meet the escaping Indians. It was Gibbon's force that came upon the Nez Percé camp in the Big Hole Valley. Yet another battle now took place between the Indians and the soldiers.

Again the Indians were taken by surprise. The soldiers charged suddenly into their camp. Once more the warriors resisted fiercely. They drove the soldiers back, pinning them down for many hours while Chief Joseph organised the escape of the Nez Percé people and their horses. The warriors managed to capture Gibbon's howitzer, which was sent crashing over a steep cliff, and 2,000 rounds of ammunition. During the fight thirty-three soldiers were killed. This time, however, the Nez Percés suffered serious losses themselves. Between sixty and ninety warriors died, including Rainbow and Five Wounds, who had sworn to die together when their time came.

Once their families were safe the warriors withdrew from the battle and rode hard after them. New decisions had to be taken. No one now listened to Looking Grass. He had said that the white people in the Big Hole Valley were friendly and that there would be no more fighting. But who could lead them? Rainbow and Five Wounds were dead. A new leader, however, was at hand. His name was Lean Elk and he had joined the tribe in the Bitterroot Valley. Lean Elk was half French and he had spent a lot of his time in the frontier towns of the west. To the whites he was known as Poker Joe because of his fondness for a card game called poker. Not only was Lean Elk a tough fighter, he also had an excellent knowledge of the area the Nez Percés were now crossing.

Led by Lean Elk the Nez Percés, with their families, possessions and animals, now hurried eastwards. Their plan was to cross the Targhee Pass into the Yellowstone area, and then head north through the buffalo country to Canada. Their retreat continued to be a fighting one. Howard was close behind them as they neared Targhee Pass. A small band of warriors led by Ollokot, Looking Glass and Tulhulhutsut, went back along the trail, attacked Howard's camp, and stampeded 200 mules. The Indians were pursued by troops but they fought them off.

The Nez Percés then headed north for Canada. During this time they fought off another army attack, raided a military depot, and defeated the Crow Indians who proved not to be friendly allies.

Only 50 kilometres from Canada, after a forced march of about 1500 kilometres the Nez Percés stopped to rest on the north side of Bear Paw Mountains. Again they believed they were safe from attack, that the soldiers were far behind. But they were wrong.

The white man had an invention that the Indian did not know about or understand. By telegraph Colonel Nelson Miles

A picture of Nelson A. Miles when he became a general

received orders to move north-west across Montana to try and catch the Indians before they reached the Canadian border.

Pushing his 600 infantrymen and horse soldiers hard Miles reached the Bear Paw Mountains at the end of September 1877. There, on a cold and windy day, his scouts spotted the Nez Percé tipis in the hollow near Snake Creek. Miles decided to attack immediately.

As the soldiers charged across the grassy plains the Nez Percés again were caught by surprise. Some of them ran away over the plains while others, including Chief Joseph, were caught with the horses some distance from the main camp. The Indians could not stop the soldiers from stampeding their herds. Chief Joseph and others waited for the darkness and then crawled back to the main camp.

Meanwhile, those in the tipis at the time of the charge had taken cover behind boulders along a low lying ridge. Firing very 69

A Remington painting showing how he thought the surrender of Chief Joseph might have looked

accurately these warriors had brought Miles's main charge to a standstill. The Nez Percés marksmen had killed twenty-four soldiers and wounded another forty-two. Unfortunately for them, however, the army had killed Ollokot and Tulhulhutsut.

Afraid to make another charge Miles now decided to lay siege to the Indians. It proved a very hard night for both sides. Five inches of snow fell, and it turned very cold. The Indians endured in the open, with no fires and tipis to keep them warm.

The next day Miles showed the white flag and Chief Joseph went into the army trenches to talk with him. Miles then captured the Chief but was forced to release him the next day in exchange for one of his officers who had been caught by the Nez Percé warriors.

70   The siege, the snow and the cold continued. Then, on 4

October, Howard reached the battlefield. The soldiers had been reinforced. The Nez Percés lost heart. Downcast, they met with their remaining leaders to decide what to do. Looking Glass still opposed surrender. Chief Joseph, however, said that their women and children were dying from the cold and hunger. He felt they must give in. Suddenly, as the meeting broke up, Looking Glass was killed by a shot in the head. Grieving, Chief Joseph got on his horse, rode slowly across to Miles's trenches, dismounted and handed his rifle to the colonel. Speaking to Miles he said:

Tell General Howard I know his heart. What he told me before I have in my heart. I am tired of fighting. Our chiefs are killed. Looking Glass is dead. Tulhulhutsut is dead. The old men are all dead. It is the young men who say yes or no. He who led the young men is dead. It is cold and we have no blankets. The little children are freezing to death. My people, some of them, have run away to the hills, and have no blankets, no food; no one knows where they are-perhaps freezing to death. I want to have time to look for my children and see how many I can find. Maybe I shall find them among the dead. Hear me, my chiefs. I am tired, my heart is sick and sad. From where the sun now stands, I will fight no more forever.

7 Red Cloud, Sitting Bull and Crazy Horse

Gold miners swarmed across the Powder River country in the early 1860s. Big strikes were made at Bannack, Alder Gulch, and Last Chance Gulch between 1862 and 1864. In one year ten million dollars worth of gold was taken from Alder Gulch. Within two years ten thousand people lived there. The site was renamed Virginia City. In 1863 wagon-loads of mining tools, food, whisky, pianos and women started to rattle and creak along the Bozeman Trail, which connected these Montana gold fields to Fort Laramie and Julesburg to the south-east.

About the same time the Union Pacific Railroad Company began to build across Nebraska, the tracks quickly appearing along the North Platte Valley to Julesburg. Like the mining towns in Montana, the railroad Company sent out hunters on the plains to kill the buffalo for food. Later, when the railroad was built, the settlers would come.

The Teton Sioux grew angry and alarmed by these events. The Powder River country and the Yellowstone valley were the heartlands of their hunting grounds. They attacked and destroyed the wagon trains making for Virginia City. In 1865 the soldiers came, to reinforce their post at Fort Laramie, and to protect the miners along the Bozeman Trail. The Sioux, led by Red Cloud, drove them away.

A year later, the soldiers came again. At Fort Laramie Red Cloud told Colonel Carrington, the commanding officer:

> You are the White Eagle who has come to steal the road. The Great Father sends us presents and wants us to sell him the road but the White Chief comes with soldiers to steal it before the Indian says yes or no. I will talk with you no

Left: *Colonel Carrington*

Below: *Fort Phil Kearny*

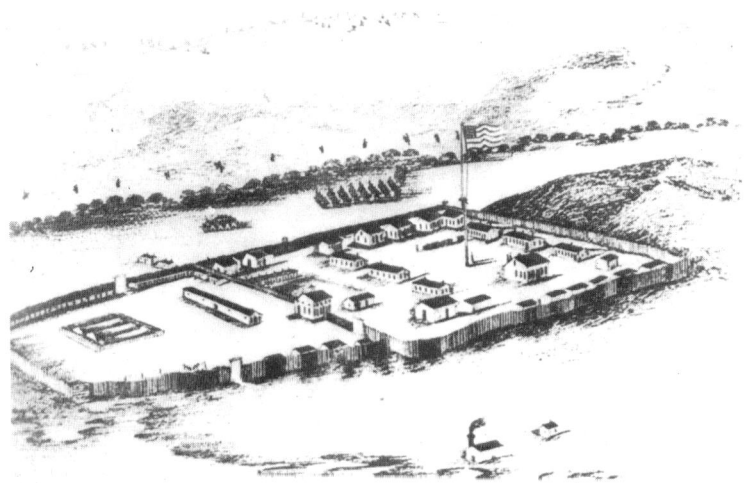

more. I will go, now, and I will fight you. As long as I live
I will fight you for the last hunting grounds of my people.

Carrington marched his seven hundred soldiers to the
Powder River. His expedition possessed a forty-piece brass
band, some rocking chairs, mowing machines, tools, a small
herd of cattle, some pigs and chickens – but it was short of
ammunition. In the next six or seven months the soldiers
occupied Fort Connor (renamed Fort Reno) and built two new
ones, Fort Phil Kearny and Fort C.F. Smith.

Map 10 shows the activities of the Americans in Sioux 73

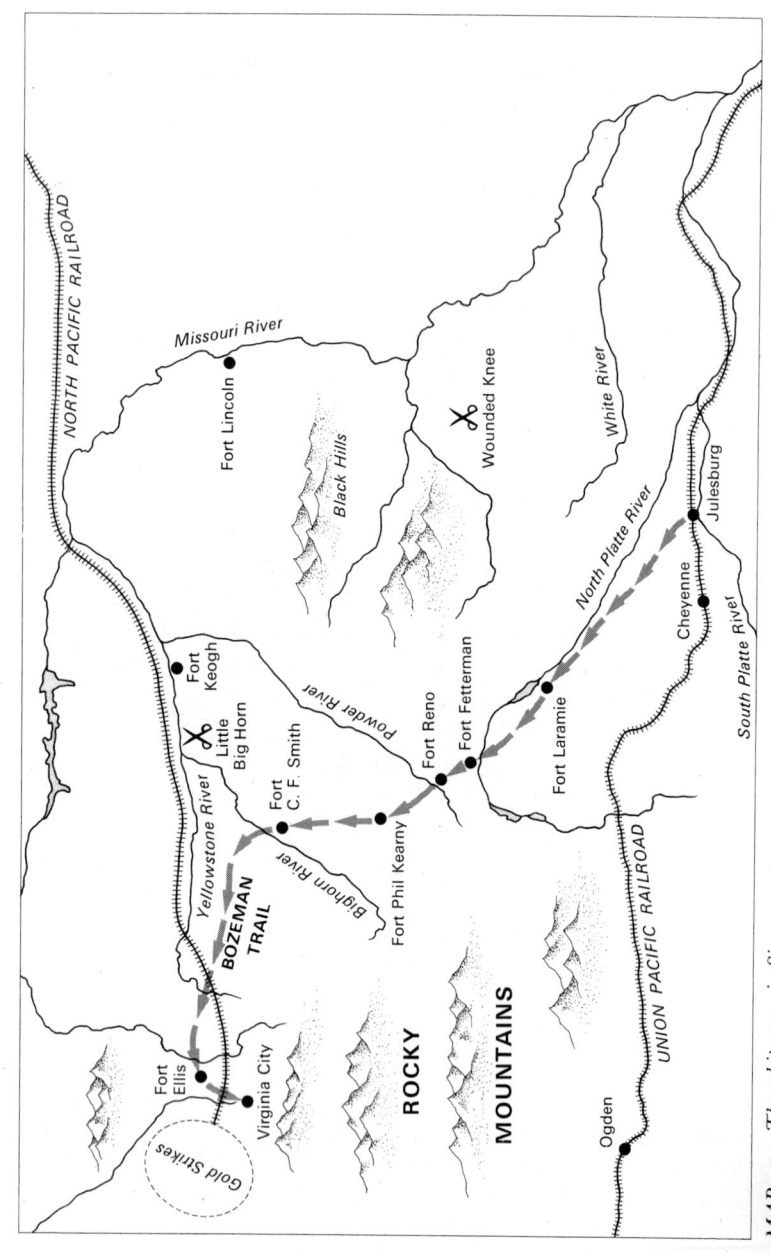

NORTH PACIFIC RAILROAD

Missouri River

Fort Lincoln

Black Hills

Wounded Knee

White River

North Platte River

Julesburg

Cheyenne

South Platte River

Fort Keogh

Little Big Horn

Powder River

Fort Reno

Fort Fetterman

Fort Laramie

Yellowstone River

Fort C. F. Smith

Fort Phil Kearny

Bighorn River

BOZEMAN TRAIL

ROCKY

MOUNTAINS

UNION PACIFIC RAILROAD

Ogden

Fort Ellis

Virginia City

Gold Strikes

MAP 10   *The white man in Sioux country*

country. It will help you to follow the story in the following few pages.

Scouts kept Red Cloud informed of the soldiers' movements. The Indians signalled each other with white flags and mirrors. White men were ambushed or picked off by snipers along the trail and outside the forts. Army horses and mules were run off. Cattle were stolen. Even the mowing machines were set on fire. Altogether fifty-one attacks were made on Fort Phil Kearny in 1866.

But the Indians were not yet ready for a mass attack on the soldiers. Autumn was the time for buffalo-hunting rather than war. Red Cloud, too, had to win allies. He turned to the Crows and the Cheyennes who lived next to the Sioux. (The map in the front inside cover shows where they lived.) The Crows refused to fight with him. In the past the Sioux had driven them from their hunting grounds and they had not forgotten this. The Cheyennes were impressed by the new fort at Phil Kearny and they knew it had been reinforced by more soldiers. But, since his speech at Fort Laramie, Red Cloud's reputation had grown. By December about two thousand Sioux and Cheyenne braves were ready to follow him against Carrington.

On a warm sunny day, four days before Christmas 1866, Red Cloud moved his warriors to Lodge Trail Ridge, not far from Fort Phil Kearny but out of sight of its look-outs. Men from the fort were out in the forests gathering wood. Red Cloud's plan was to attack the woodcutters and draw soldiers from the fort to rescue the party. The soldiers would then be *decoyed* by a war party to be led by a young war chief, Crazy Horse, towards Lodge Trail Ridge where most of the warriors would be hidden. The plan worked perfectly.

As soon as the woodcutters were attacked, Carrington sent out eighty men under Captain Fetterman. Leaving the fort Fetterman was twice told by Carrington not to pursue the Indians over Lodge Trail Ridge. But Fetterman thought little of the Indians' fighting ability and he said publicly that 'with eighty men I could ride through the Sioux nation'. Eager for battle, his chance had come.

As he approached the scene of the attack the Indians withdrew. Suddenly, Crazy Horse and his warriors dashed out of the brush, yelling and waving blankets to frighten the soldiers' horses. The Indians crossed in front of Fetterman and then retreated slowly towards the ridge. Angry, the captain waved his men to follow them. From behind rocks and from the brush Red Cloud's warriors rushed in on the whites. War clubs hit rifle butts. The foot soldiers ran behind some large flat stones. A rain of arrows killed them all. The mounted soldiers swung up a snow-covered hill. They fired their *muzzle-loading* rifles. As they stopped to re-load, the Indians charged and slew them.

Great became the fame of Red Cloud. In 1867 he determined to drive out the whites completely. While the Cheyennes attacked Fort C.F. Smith, his Sioux warriors returned to Fort Phil Kearny. Covered in white, yellow and green warpaint, their plan was to repeat the one of 1866; but this time it did not work. The soldiers now had Springfield *breech-loading rifles*. Crouching behind wagon horses, the soldiers refused to be decoyed by Crazy Horse. Red Cloud waited until the soldiers fired their first round and then he attacked. To his amazement the soldiers kept firing. They no longer needed to reload after each shot. Red Cloud saw many of his best warriors killed. With the approach of a relief party with howitzer guns he decided to call off his attack. The Cheyennes met a similar fate at Fort C.F. Smith.

Red Cloud believed he had lost the battle. His resistance to the white man, however, led the government to rethink its policy along the Bozeman Trail. By April 1868 a peace treaty was ready for Red Cloud's signature. The Treaty began: 'From this day forward all war between the parties to this agreement shall forever cease.' The soldiers were withdrawn from Fort Phil Kearny, Fort Reno, and Fort C.F. Smith. The Indians burned down the buildings. Red Cloud believed he had won back the Sioux hunting grounds. He took his followers to the Powder River country to enjoy the hunting and live in peace.

In 1870 Red Cloud, Spotted Tail and other chiefs were
invited to Washington for talks. For the first time Red Cloud

Above: *A painting of an Indian watching over a captive trooper*

Left: *A photograph of Red Cloud taken in 1884, after his victories over the Americans*

77

saw how strong the white man was, in numbers and resources. He reported his demands: 'When we first had this land we were strong, but now we are melting like snow on the hillside, while you are grown like spring grass. I have two mountains in that country, the Black Hills and the Big Horn Mountains. I want the Father to make no roads through them.'

The whites, however, made it clear that they expected Red Cloud to live in peace and to settle on land specially reserved for him by the government in South Dakota. The Indians would be trained by agents for a farming way of life. Red Cloud and Spotted Tail agreed to these terms. In 1871 Red Cloud and his followers left the Powder River country and settled down on a new agency near Fort Laramie. Spotted Tail moved to one near the Upper White River. You can see where these places were by looking at Map 11 on page 84.

Red Cloud did not speak for all the Sioux. Many of them now lost confidence in him. They turned to men like Sitting Bull and Crazy Horse, who rejected the treaty and chose to fight on against any white trespasser on the Powder River and Yellowstone country.

The white man was not long in coming. In 1871 surveyors for the Northern Pacific Railroad entered the Yellowstone valley. They were protected by soldiers under the command of George Custer. In 1874 Custer was sent to *reconnoitre* the Black Hills. A fort built there, it was believed, would make it easier to protect the railroad.

Unexpectedly, Custer's men found gold. A new gold rush began. Indians and miners killed each other. Miners began offering two hundred dollars for every Indian scalp taken. The Government held a council with the Sioux at Red Cloud's reservation near Fort Laramie. It tried to make them sell the Black Hills. Red Cloud demanded six hundred million dollars for the land. None of the Oglala and Hunkpapa tribes attended the council and Crazy Horse said: 'One does not sell the earth upon which people walk.' To the government the only thing to do was to keep the Sioux inside their reservations. In December 1875 it issued an order that all Indians not on the

*An engraving of Sitting Bull
made in 1886*

reservation by 31 January 1876 would be considered enemies. Crazy Horse and Sitting Bull, and their Cheyennes allies, prepared for war.

In April 1876 Sitting Bull called a great council at Chalk Buttes on the Tongue River. Crazy Horse was there, and so were many Cheyennes and Arapahoes. (The Arapahoes lived along the South Platte River. Like the Sioux and the Cheyennes they were alarmed by the activities of miners and railroadmen.) Everybody talked of war. After the spring hunts in the Rosebud country, the Indians set up a new camp at Ash Creek. A great sun dance was held. Sitting Bull sought a vision. From his arms were cut a hundred small pieces of flesh. Bleeding, he danced all day until he fell exhausted and unconscious. When he recovered he told the Indians his vision: he had seen many soldiers coming into camp upside down. The warriors were pleased. They would win the war.

By this time three army columns were on their way to the Powder River. General Crook's column was first into the area but it was beaten back by Crazy Horse and the Oglalas. The other two columns of soldiers met at the mouth of the Powder.

General Terry decided to send 400 infantry under General Gibbon up the Big Horn River. The much faster 7th Cavalry, under George Custer, was sent along the Powder River, where Indian trails had been sighted. Terry believed the Sioux were camped in the valley of the Little Big Horn. If so, his plan was to catch Crazy Horse and Sitting Bull between Gibbon's and Custer's detachments.

Custer pushed his men hard up the Powder valley. He was confident that his cavalry could outfight any band of Indians. When his scouts reported an Indian encampment in the Little Big Horn Valley he decided to attack from the front. Custer split his men into three groups. The first group was sent to the left to scout the ridges: the second, under Major Reno, was to move directly forward. Custer led the third group to the right. Reno met fierce resistance and was pinned down for a day or so. The first group joined him later. Custer, meanwhile, was charged by Crazy Horse. In half an hour Custer and his two hundred and twenty-five men were all dead.

Here is a short account of the battle at the Little Big Horn, written some time after it was all over by an Indian who took part in the battle:

> There was not much excitement and at first we thought it would be better to surrender as there were so many soldiers in this country, but when Custer came in sight there were not so many, and the word was sent around the camp to get ready. We sneaked from our tents through the tall grass to where our ponies were picketed [tied up] and drew them to us by the long ropes. . . .We raced towards the soldiers as the bullets came switching through the grass and through the leaves of the trees. But we were not excited.
>
> And we fought, and the soldiers fought, and when we chased the first lot across the river we turned and went for those on the hills. The smoke and dust were very thick – you couldn't see anything and we killed lots of our own men

Left: *One of the many painting of Custer's Last Stand at the Battle of Little Big Horn. It is not accurate in every detail. For example, historians know from written records that Custer was armed with two revolvers. He did not carry a sabre*

because they got in the way.

Pretty soon the soldiers began to run and we went after them but it wasn't long before they were all killed or wounded. We couldn't tell who was Custer, we couldn't tell anything; their faces were covered with dust and their eyes and mouths were full of it. . . .

We dressed ourselves in the uniforms and put on the swords and took the flags and bugles and marched around, and we marched toward Reno that way, too. And Reno was up on a hill across from our camp and his men were lying in trenches and they didn't have any water all day and it was very hot. Once in a while a soldier would start down the bluff, sneaking through the grass. He'd stop and be still and then he'd crawl along again and we'd let him get pretty close to the river's edge and we'd shoot him. Once a soldier got clear down to the water and drank and filled some round things with stoppers in them with water, and started back, but we played with him and shot him.

The soldiers had lots of money and we took it. We knew what the silver was but the paper we didn't know. And the children played with it; they made little tipis out of it . . . . . and some of it was bloody.

And after we saw what we had done some of us thought we would get hanged and some of us thought we would not get any rations if we went back to the reservations, and we heard that the country was full of more white soldiers coming, and we were all scared, so we broke camp next day and left. . . .

We brought our wounded with us and they died along the way and we buried them and our hearts were bad. The women also buried lots of trinkets, like rings and things that we took from the dead soldiers, because we were scared.

We had done more than we thought we ever could do, and we knew that the whites were very strong and would punish us.

All America was thunderstruck by Custer's death. The people insisted on sending a large army to defeat the Sioux once and for all. Crook's army was heavily reinforced and the soldiers armed with Gatling guns. The boundaries of the Sioux reservation in Dakota were reduced. The Black Hills now belonged to the Americans. Red Cloud reluctantly agreed to this new treaty, on behalf of the peaceful Indians.

Sitting Bull led his people to the Yellowstone, hunted for a while, and then went north into Canada rather than surrender to the soldiers. Crazy Horse went first to the Powder River and then to the Tongue. His camp was found by Crook and a big battle was fought. Luckily for Crazy Horse a blinding snowstorm came and he was able to move his Oglalas away, the storm hiding his movements. The soldiers returned to their fort. The Indians stayed out in the snow, cold and hungry. Crazy Horse knew he could not last out much longer.

Hearing of a promise of a reservation in buffalo country, Crazy Horse decided to lead his people to the reservation. The procession was 3 kilometres long, the warriors first and then the women and children, the packhorses and the dogs, the travois and the folded tipis. The soldiers took away from them over two thousand four hundred horses and a hundred and seventeen guns. It was May 1877.

But there was no reservation in buffalo country. Crazy Horse grew restless. The soldiers and Indian scouts watched him closely. Was he planning to break away and take his Oglalas with him? They decided to arrest him and put him in the guard house. Crazy Horse struggled to resist. He was bayoneted to death 'while trying to escape', the army report said. So died the greatest Sioux war chief, a man who had never lost a battle to the white soldiers.

Meanwhile, in Canada, Sitting Bull and his Hunkpapas were facing hardships. The Canadian settlers were frightened by his presence. The Canadian goverment would not give him a reservation. The buffalo were fast disappearing from the plains, killed by miners, railroad companies and hunters seeking hides and furs for the eastern markets. In 1840 it was said that forty million buffalo roamed the plains. By 1880 only about one million remained and the white man continued to kill them

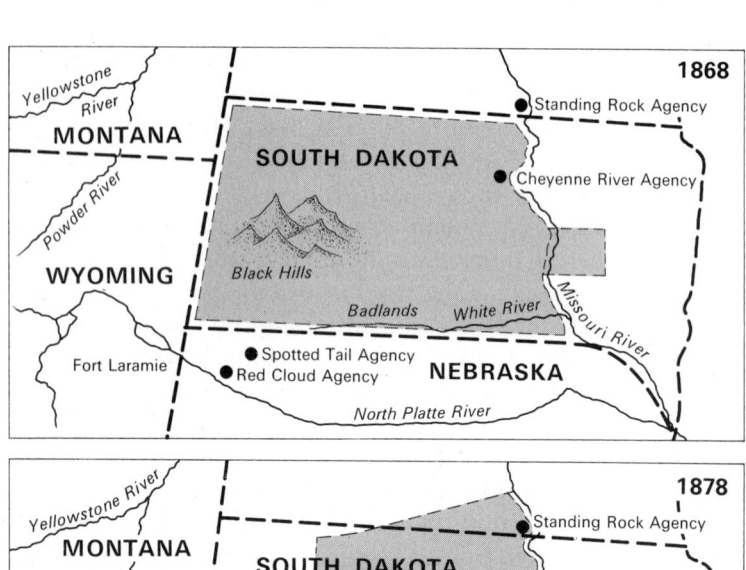

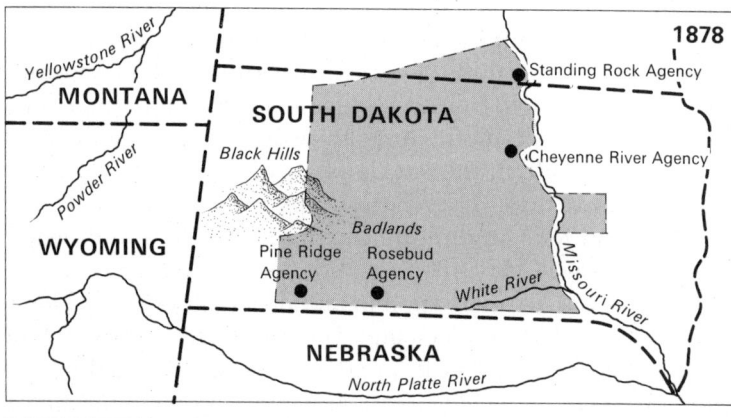

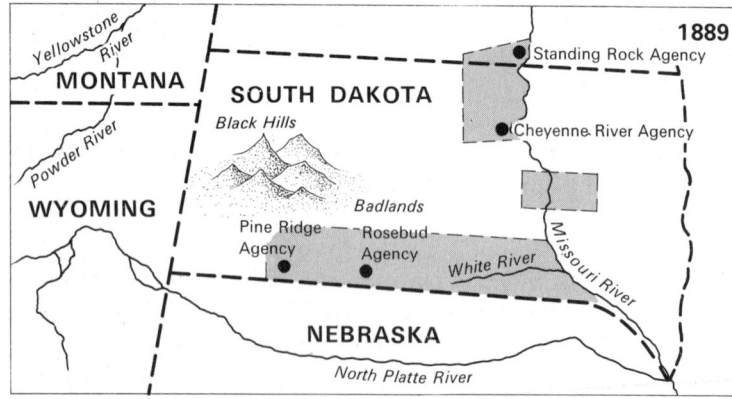

remorselessly, leaving the prairies strewn with their bones. Sitting Bull surrendered to the Americans in 1881. His followers went to the Standing Rock Agency. He himself was put in gaol at Fort Randal and stayed there for two years.

When he was set free Sitting Bull went to live with his people in Standing Rock. From the beginning he became a thorn in the side of the agent and the politicians. He repeatedly asked for better living conditions for the Hunkpapas, and firmly opposed any further cuts in size of the Sioux reservation.

Despite Sitting Bull's efforts, however, the Sioux suffered a further drastic cut in their land when, in 1889, a large area about 80 kilometres wide in the centre of the reservation was taken from them. This division of the reservation was to allow the miners and other whites to reach the Black Hills without having first to cross Sioux land. Map 11 shows the Sioux reservation after the 1889 treaty. Other chiefs, who signed the treaty, were not so stubborn and determined as Sitting Bull to preserve the Sioux land. When he heard of the signing of the treaty he said: 'I am the only Sioux left.'

The condition of the Sioux worsened rapidly in 1889 and 1890. Not only were the buffalo gone, and their lands much smaller than ever before, but dry winds ruined their crops, their monthly beef rations had been cut by more than half, and many families suffered from measles, influenza and whooping cough.

Defeated in war and their nomadic life ended, the Sioux were low in spirit, without hope or purpose. In 1889, however, they heard rumours about an Indian sent from God with good news for all Indians, a man who prophesied the return of their old way of life. Were these rumours true? Who was this prophet? The Sioux sent men to find out.

On their return they had a wonderful story to tell. The Indian that was spoken of was a Paiute sheep-herder named Wovoka. During an eclipse of the sun, when 'the sun was dead', Wovoka had had a vision. He rose to heaven and saw God and

MAP 11   These maps show how the Sioux reservation land (the shaded areas) grew less and less between 1868 to 1889 as it was taken away from them

all the Indians who had lived long ago. God gave him a message to tell all the Indians on earth. Soon the earth would tremble. The Indians then must put their sacred feathers into their hair so that they could fly into the sky while a new earth replaced the old. No white man would be on this new land. When the Indians came down from the sky they would find their dead relatives and ancestors all restored to life. The buffalo would be everywhere. There would be no more hunger, sickness, pain or death. This new life was coming soon: in the spring of 1891. At regular intervals the Indians must perform the Ghost Dance. By dancing and praying, Wovoka said, Indians could 'die' for a few moments and enjoy a brief visit to this new land to see what it looked like.

Old Red Cloud did not accept this new religion. Sitting Bull did, and he took part in the Ghost Dances at Standing Rock. Ghost Dancers appeared elsewhere on the reservation, particularly at the Pine Ridge and Rosebud agencies. Wovoka had said that Ghost Dancing must be peaceful but the Sioux made it into a war dance. They claimed that their Ghost shirts were bullet-proof and, as their enthusiasm for the Dance grew, many of them danced with rifles in their hands.

Before they danced the Sioux cleansed their bodies and souls by taking sweat baths in small dome-shaped huts made from willow branches and skins. The medicine men passed hot stones into the huts and the Indians inside poured cold water over them causing great clouds of steam. At noon, the dancing began. Each dancer had his face painted with circles, crescents and crosses which represented the sun, moon, and stars. These designs were painted, too, on their fringed shirts which were made of cotton cloth or muslin. The shirts were decorated with feathers as well. In their hair the dancers wore eagle feathers, which would allow them to fly up into the air when the time for the great revolution came.

The agent at Pine Ridge, new to the job and knowing little about the Sioux, grew frightened by the Ghost dancers. He sent for the soldiers. With their coming, thousands of Sioux fled to the Badlands at the western edge of the Pine Ridge area to

Remington's painting of the Ghost Dance by Oglala Sioux

hide. An army order was given for the arrest of Sitting Bull. The agent at Standing Rock insisted that Sitting Bull should be arrested by the Indian police, not the soldiers. He believed it would cause less trouble. He was wrong.

Sitting Bull was asleep in his log cabin when the police arrived. He agreed to leave peacefully, but his followers gathered around the cabin door, jostling the police. A shot was fired at the policeman in charge who then fired at Sitting Bull and killed him.

Fearful of real trouble now, the army ordered a careful watch on other Indian leaders, particularly a man called Big Foot, who was camped along the Cheyenne River. This alarmed Big Foot who, with his band, also fled towards the Badlands. But his band was caught by the soldiers and escorted to a small settlement called Wounded Knee.

Camped down for the night the Indians were surrounded by four hundred and seventy men armed with rifles and within range of four *hotchkiss* guns stationed on a small hill overlooking the camp. A white flag flew above Big Foot's tipi.

In the morning the soldiers moved across the snow to disarm 87

The frozen corpse of Big Foot. This photograph was taken at Wounded Knee just after the massacre. No other corpses can be seen although there were many of them. Did this photographer miss them out on purpose so that the American whites would not see the terrible slaughter done by their soldiers?

the Indians, who numbered a hundred and six men and two hundred and twenty-four women and children. The warriors were unwilling to surrender their weapons and the soldiers were told to enter the tipis and find them. About forty guns were found. Then, suddenly, one Indian raised a gun from beneath his blanket and fired at the soldiers. The troops replied instantly and half of the warriors fell dead. The remaining men grappled with the soldiers, fighting hand to hand using knives and clubs drawn from below their blankets. The hotchkiss guns now fired on the women and children, who had been made to stand aside while the search for guns was made.

Within minutes two hundred Indians and sixty soldiers lay dead or wounded. Women and children who ran away were shot down, and some who hid were killed when they were seen. By the end perhaps three hundred Indians had died at the hands of the soldiers from the 7th Cavalry – Custer's regiment.

On New Year's Day 1891, three days after the killings, the dead Indians were buried naked in a long pit. Their Ghost shirts were ripped off them by souvenir hunters. The Sioux no longer believed in Wovoka and the coming of the new world. At Wounded Knee lay buried not only three hundred Indians 88 but the hopes and dreams of the whole Sioux nation.

8   Postscript

In the few days following the slaughter at Wounded Knee angry Sioux warriors attacked troops and wagon trains. The soldiers encircled them and pushed them back to the reservation. By 16 January all the warriors had given up.

For the fighting Nez Percés and Apaches defeat was even more bitter than for the Sioux. But it was not to be. They were sent first to an unhealthy swamp near Fort Leavenworth where twenty-one of them died from disease in the seven months they were there. Later, the Nez Percés were taken to a hot and dry reserve in Kansas Territory where another forty-seven Indians died. Chief Joseph, now famous throughout America for his fighting retreat, his poetic speech of surrender, and his great moral courage, protested about the government's treatment of his people. The Nez Percés were a people of the cool mountains and forests of the north-west. From Kansas his people were then moved to Oklahoma, but still things were no better. Almost every child that was born there died. Finally, in 1885, a hundred and eighteen of the Nez Percés were allowed to return to their reservation at Lapwai.

The Apaches, too, were treated badly by the American government. Geronimo, Nana and many of the Chiricahuas and Mimbrenos from the San Carlos reservation, were sent by train to Florida. Even the Apache scouts who had helped Crook and Miles to defeat Geronimo were sent there too. The damp climate soon killed off dozens of the Indians. In 1886 a group of five hundred and two Apaches arrived at Fort Marion. By 1887 only four hundred and forty-seven remained alive. From Florida they were packed off first to Alabama and then, in 1894, to Fort Sill, in Oklahoma. By this time only four hundred and seven remained. The fighting Apaches were kept at Fort Sill for nearly twenty years. Not until 1913 was the way open for them to return to their homeland. Then a hundred and eighty-seven people chose to go and live at the Mescalero reservation near Fort Stanton. Nearly a hundred Apaches decided to stay at Fort Sill. You can see all these movements on map 12 inside the back cover of this book.

But even reservations in their homeland was a cruel fate for the fighting Indians of the American West. To live in a confined space, to farm thin soils with meagre tools and low skills, to make weekly visits to the government agency to receive rations of food and blankets – these were not their ways of living.

Today, about half a million Indians live in towns. For example, there are Sioux living in Denver and Omaha, Apaches in Phoenix and Tucson, and Nez Percés in Lewiston. Nearly the same number live on reservations. Life there remains hard. Reservation Indians are the poorest, the unhealthiest, the least educated, and the lowest employed of all American citizens. White men continue to want their land, water, timber and minerals.

A poor Apache family in Mexico in 1938

Recently there has been trouble at the Pine Ridge reservation in S. Dakota. Some Oglala Sioux (both Sitting Bull and Crazy Horse belonged to this tribe) complained that people with white men's blood in them were governing the reservation and mis-using tribal money. They staged a protest and chose Wounded Knee as the place to make it. Perhaps you can think why they should choose this village? Federal marshals surrounded it and during several exchanges of gunfire two Indians were killed and one policeman wounded.

Some reservations have seen improvements since 1945. For example, the Apaches have used their land for cattle ranching and forestry. The government has opened recreation areas nearby and the Apaches have started stores and shops to cater for the white holiday-makers. With better jobs and more money these Indians have bought themselves cars and trucks and household goods like refrigerators and television sets. At the Rosebud reservation, Brule Sioux hire themselves out as labourers to white farmers nearby, living away from the reservation during spring and summer but returning there for the winter. At times, too, many have worked as film extras for Hollywood companies making Westerns in the Black Hills.

Yet such improvements are only the beginning. Today, Indians from many tribes are members of an organisation known as the American Indian Movement (AIM). It wants the federal government to observe properly all the existing treaties between itself and the Indian tribes. Reservation lands must be guaranteed to the Indians. Their water, trees and minerals must be protected from greedy white men. The government must provide better schools and medical services for the tribes. And, very important, argues AIM, Indians must be allowed to run their own lands and direct their own lives.

America still has an Indian problem. Placing Indians on reservations and then forgetting them was no final solution. A century after Crazy Horse, Chief Joseph and Victorio, the Sioux, the Nez Percés and the Apaches are still struggling for their survival and for their future.

How Do We Know?

From the very beginning of their contact with the Indians white men have recorded the details of how the tribes lived and the wars which took place between them. For example, Lewis and Clark travelled amongst the Sioux and the Nez Percés and wrote about them in their journals. Soldiers who lived with and fought against the Indians have written books about their experiences. Francis Parkman, a young student, rode out on the high plains in 1846 and wrote what has become a very famous book, 'The Oregon Trail', which says a great deal about the Sioux before they fought against the whites. Portraits of Indians were painted by great artists like Karl Bodmer, George Catlin, Seth Eastman and Frederick Remington. Some of their pictures are in this book. They are important historical documents on Indian life. Speeches made by Indian leaders like Red Cloud, Sitting Bull and Chief Joseph were written down at the time they were spoken. They survive today for us to read. Two Apaches, James Kaywaykla and Jason Betzinez, described their early life when they were on the warpath with Victorio and Geronimo. American museums, of course, have many exhibits of clothes, utensils, tools, weapons and paintings which belonged to the Indians.

The two books mentioned in To the Reader and the following will help you to find out more.

BALL, E. *The Last Days of Victorio,*

BEACROFT, B.W. and SMALE, M.A. *The Making of America,* Longman, 1972

BETZINEZ, J. *I Fought with Geronimo,* Stackpole, 1960

CHALMERS, H. *Last Stand of the Nez Percés,* Twayne, 1962

ELLACOT, S.E. *Guns,* Methuen, 1955

GORHAM, M. *Real Book of Red Indians,* Dobson, 1958

HUNT, W.B. *Golden Book of Indian Crafts and Lore,* Publicity, 1954

LA FARGE, O. *A Pictorial History of the American Indian,* Spring, 1956

REMINGTON, F. *Frederick Remington's Own West,* Foulsham, 1960

SANDOZ, M. *These were the Sioux,* Hastings, 1961.

And there is a good filmstrip:

Common Ground, *The Westward Movement,* Longman, 1976.

Things To Do

1. Study the picture on page 23 and read the description of the buffalo hunt on page 22. Imagine you are taking part in a buffalo hunt and write an account of your expedition.
2. Read page 36 and make a painting of the vision of Crazy Horse.
3. Look again at the illustrations in chapters 1 and 5 and re-read chapter 5. Pretend you are a white miner or settler in Apache country and either write a petition to the American Army or a letter to an Arizona newspaper stating your reasons for demanding the soldiers' protection from Apache raids.
4. Paintings, drawings and photographs can be both reliable and unreliable as sources of historical information. Discuss this in class, using the pictures in this book as evidence. Study in particular those on pages 8, 11, 17, 21, 23, 26, 37, 55, 70, 80, 88 and 90.
5. Some people think that Chief Joseph was one of the greatest of all Indian leaders. They say he was intelligent, wise, patient and courageous. What examples would you give to support these ideas?
6. Americans have said that the events at the Little Big Horn were a massacre and those at Wounded Knee a battle. Indians have said that the Little Big Horn was a battle and Wounded Knee a massacre. What are your opinions? (See pages 81, 82, 87 and 88).
7. (a) Imagine you were one of the Indian war chiefs mentioned in this book. Make up a speech to deliver to your class giving the reasons why you intend to fight the white men and drive them out of your homeland.
   (b) Imagine you were one of the peaceful Indians and make up a speech to deliver to the class stating why you were not prepared to take up arms against the Americans.
8. Using the information in the first three chapters discuss in class the reasons why the Sioux, the Apaches and the Nez Percés found it so hard to settle down to live on reservations
9. Hold a debate in class: 'That this House believes there was no honourable solution to the "Indian problem" in the late nineteenth century.'
10. If you live near Bath or have an opportunity to go there, visit the American Museum at Claverton.

Glossary

agent, a person authorised by the government to act on its behalf
to anticipate, to realise or know beforehand
assailant, attacker
bluff, high steep bank of a river
box canyon, a deep gorge sealed or closed at one end. See also *canyon*
breechclout, a strip of buskskin leather passed between the legs from front of the waist to the back
breech-loading rifle, rifle in which the ammunition is loaded at the butt or rear end of the barrel
cache, secret hole in the ground in which to hide food, clothes, weapons, etc.
canyon, deep, narrow gorge or opening between mountains
carcass, dead body
cigarillo, cigar
commissioner, person appointed by the government to carry out a particular enquiry
concentric, having a common centre
coyote, small wolf-like animal
decoyed, lured away
dome-shaped, having a rounded top like half an orange
downwind, position in which the hunter's scent is blown away from the animal, thereby stopping it smelling the man's presence
edible, fit to eat
elk, a large member of the deer family, wintering in the valleys but living in the mountains in summer
emigrant, someone leaving home to live in another country
envoy, messenger or representative
feat, act of skill or daring
Federal government, the central government of America; it meets in Washington to represent all the American states
flag of truce, flag flown to show peaceful intentions, at least for the time being
Gatling gun, earliest form of machine gun, named after the man who invented it in 1862
guttural, a sound produced in the throat, harsh and rasping
hallucinations, things a person thinks he sees but which are not really there

heliostat, instrument which reflects the sunlight

heritage, what one receives from one's ancestors

hotchkiss gun, a light machine gun

howitzer, a short, squat gun used for shelling at a steep angle

international boundary, a line on a map which shows the borders dividing one country from another

intestine, part of the digestive system of the human body

irrigation ditches, ditches dug to bring water from a river or reservoir to the fields.

keg, small barrel

kite, bird of the hawk family

lacrosse, a team game played with a ball carried in curved and netted sticks

malaria, an infectious fever spread by mosquito bites

memento, an object kept to remind the owner of something; a keepsake

mule deer, deer with a mule-like tail and large ears, living in open forest land

muzzle-loading rifle, rifle in which the ammunition is loaded at the mouth of the barrel

posse, group of volunteers formed by a law officer to hunt down wanted men

quiver, leather case in which arrows are kept

to reconnoitre, to investigate the position and strength of the enemy

reservation, land set aside by the government for the sole use of the Indians

rod, unit of measurement; one rod equals about five metres

sinew, cord of tough tissue joining the muscles to the bones

slugs, pieces of metal for firing from a gun

squashes, large fleshy fruits; for example, pumpkins

squaws, Indian women

symbols, figures, letters, signs and emblems representing something; for example, a circle for the sun, a cross for a star

tanning fluid, an acid liquid used in making hides into leather

tarantula, large, poisonous spider

tipi, hut made by spreading animal skins over a framework of wooden poles

tiswin, an alcoholic drink made from corn; about as strong as beer

transcontinental, crossing a whole continent

tsach, Indian cradle carried on a woman's back

Wyakin, the belief of a Nez Percé Indian that he was watched over and protected by a spirit from evil and misfortune

Acknowledgements

For permission to reproduce illustrative material we are grateful to the following:

page:
7 Courtesy of the American Museum of Natural History (A.M.N.H.)
8 U.S. National Archives (U.S.N.A.)
11 Western Americana Picture Library (W.A.)
17 The Walters Art Gallery, Baltimore, Maryland
18 Smithsonian Institution (S.I.)
21 Northern Natural Gas Company Collection Joslyn Art Museum, Nebraska (N.N.G.C.)
23 W.A.
25 W.A.
26 Architect of the Capitol, Washington, D.C.
30 Photo Courtesy of John Hancock Mutual Life Insurance Company
34 N.N.G.C.
37 W.A.
41 W.A.
44 W.A.
49 A.M.N.H.

page:
51 Mrs. Eve Ball, Ruidoso, New Mexico
53 Library of Congress (L.C.)
55 U.S.N.A.
59 *above* S.I.
   below W.A.
61 U.S.N.A.
69 W.A.
70 L.C.
73 *above* U.S.N.A.
   below U.S.N.A.
77 *above* Cincinnati Art Museum Gift of Mrs. Benjamin E. Tate (formerly Mrs. Henry C. Yeiser) and Julius Fleischmann
   below U.S.N.A.
79 The Mansell Collection
80 The New York Historical Society
87 A.M.N.H.
88 S.I.
90 Photo: Associated Press

Colours

Illustrated by Colin Twinn

Purple

What colour are Susan's flowers?

One sunny day the Bunnykins
family go to the park.
Susan stops to buy some flowers.